Tolerable Good Anchorage
A Capsule History of St. John's, Newfoundland

JOAN RUSTED

Creative Publishers
St. John's, Newfoundland
1995

Appreciation is expressed to *The Canada Council* for publication assistance.

The publisher acknowledges the financial contribution of the *Department of Tourism and Culture, Government of Newfoundland and Labrador*, which has helped make this publication possible.

Cover photo: Don Lane

∝ Printed on acid-free paper

Published by
CREATIVE BOOK PUBLISHING
A Division of 10366 Newfoundland Limited
A Robinson-Blackmore Printing & Publishing associated company
P.O. Box 8660, St. John's, Newfoundland A1B 3T7

Printed in Canada by:
ROBINSON-BLACKMORE PRINTING & PUBLISHING

Canadian Cataloguing in Publication Data

Rusted, Joan, 1946–

    Tolerable good anchorage

    Includes bibliographical references.
    ISBN 1-895387-57-4

1. St. John's (Nfld.) — History. I. Title.

FC2196.4.R87 1995   971.8'1   C95-950203-3
F1124.5.S14R87 1995

To Pedro & Betna
best wishes
Joan Rusted

Tolerable Good Anchorage
A Capsule History of St. John's, Newfoundland

JOAN RUSTED

To Andrew

Table of Contents

Preface

My work with the sailing schooner J&B during the summer of 1994 with Bob and Maureen Jenkins, Captain Jim Parsons and Rhonda Richards was the impetus for this book. It was a summer never to be forgotten.

I have written this book with the hope that it may be easier to find an overview of local information on the historic background, points of interest in our oldest city in North America, our seafaring heritage and marine life - something I found difficult when researching material for a historical tour interpretation and answers to the many questions asked daily by tourists. My interest was roused to find out yet more as I searched through the enormous amount of information available. I learned of the many factors that prevented and hindered permanent settlement - or helped it in other instances, the west country merchants and adventurers that competed for supremacy for the fishery in Newfoundland waters, the conflicts between the contending groups and laws governing trade between Newfoundland and England, battles between the English and French, our contributions in both World Wars, how Confederation with Canada took place, the demise of the fishery and our outlook for the future. St. John's is a city that grew around its perfectly landlocked harbour and has spread to the north and west of the original town, its very fabric effectively its political history. It has been a centre of island life with shipping connections to Britain, the U.S. and Canada, its harbour the centre for goods and base for fishing fleets, serving as a naval base in the was of 1812 and in the two World Wars. My

1993 field study term in England exploring British social history and architecture helped my understanding of the origins of our local architecture, historic buildings and harbour fortifications.

"Tolerable Good Anchorage" is the result of my research. The title came from a description of the St. John's Harbour in the 1786 logbook of the H.M.S. *Pegasus* — "The entrance of St. John's Harbour forms a long and extremely narrow strait, but not very difficult of access. There are about twelve fathoms of water in the middle of the channel, with tolerable good anchorage ground."

Acknowledgements

Many thanks go to the following people for their help and encouragement in my project: Don Lane for the cover photograph; Joan Ritcey — Centre for Newfoundland Studies, Memorial University; Mrs. Kitty Power, Newfoundland Historical Society; Helen Miller and Fred Winsor at the St. John's City Hall Archives; Gerry Penney, for information on harbour fortifications and excavations at the St. John's Narrows; my father Dr. Nigel Rusted for the use of his library and photographs; Sam Naidu, Fisheries and Oceans Canada Research, for information on alternative fisheries; Peter Beamish for information on whales and seabirds; Hugh and Ann Schofield of Leoframes Antique Prints in Brighton England for the woodcut prints of the fishery; Dr. Jim Hiller; Dr. Shannon Ryan for his lectures that inspired me to learn more about our Newfoundland history; Dr. Peter Boswell and Dr. David Bell of Memorial University who encouraged me at university, and Denis Jenkins for his support.

CHAPTER ONE

Newfoundland History: Fishery To Colony

War and the fishery have shaped Newfoundland's history. Four nations—Spain, Portugal, France and England—each claimed a right to the migratory fishery in Newfoundland waters. England and France recognised the benefit of the fishery as a "nursery for seamen" – a source of trained men for their navies in wartime. Newfoundland's rich fishery and its geographic position at the gateway to North America made it an important region in international diplomacy and balance of power.

The Renaissance brought about many technological changes enabling European ships to explore new lands. John Cabot sailed from Bristol, England in 1497, landing in North America on the 24th of June, the feast day of St. John the Baptist – from which came the name of St. John's. As no charts or documents of Cabot's voyages exist today, the exact site of his landfall is debatable and is thought to have been either in Newfoundland or Cape Breton, but theories about latitude sailing make the landfall most likely in Newfoundland. In 1583 Sir Humphrey Gilbert arrived with three ships and claimed the colony for England in the name of Queen Elizabeth.

Western Europe's expansion into the new world began in the 15th century when Spain and Portugal founded colonies in

South America for exploitation and financial gain. The fishery brought about a different kind of wealth in the 16th century and the island of Newfoundland became a source of rivalry amongst Spanish, Portuguese, French and English fishermen. The four countries worked out an informal admiralty system to establish order in the harbours, and by 1570 are reputed to have rotated this system amongst the nations. This period has been called the commercial and non-political phase of Newfoundland's history. England's fishery was at first not a national enterprise but was controlled by the merchants of its West Country, southwest coastal England, as a private venture for profit. This gave the West Country the key to England's naval strength. Each year, West Country sailors went to the Newfoundland fishery, then to Portugal, Spain and home, gaining valuable seafaring experience in the harsh Atlantic. In contrast, the sailors from London mainly sailed to France and Belgium, not gaining this experience. Soon the British authorities began to see the cod fishery as a basis of naval strength, a means of getting a share of Spanish and Portuguese wealth in markets for fish, and as a way to increase the revenues of the government with tariffs.

THE IMPACT OF WAR

England was involved in sixteen wars between the year of the Spanish Armada in 1588 and the end of the Napoleonic Wars in 1815. Many of these wars had an impact upon Newfoundland, and the future of the island hung more upon the result of wars in Europe than on any local battles.

The defeat of the Spanish Armada gave England control of the transatlantic codfishery. It marked the end of the Spanish fishery but not the end of Spain's power at sea, which was to menace British shipping for many years to come. The decline in the Spanish fishery created a demand for salt fish, which gave England a great opportunity. Only the French and English were left participants in the fishery – as competitors.

The Civil Wars in England from 1642-48 were devastating for the Newfoundland fishery, with pirates and Commonwealth cruisers seriously affecting trade and industry. The West Country fishery declined from about 270 vessels during the reign of James I to about 199 in this period. Oliver Cromwell's policy was one of Protector to Newfoundland, sending ships to protect the fishery. The first real governor of the island was appointed. The governor formerly had been just a manager of a colonization company with no direct commission from the Crown. Newfoundland ships, protected by their escort, traded with Gibraltar, where the fish was later smuggled into Spain and sold.

The Dutch wars followed four years after the Restoration of the monarchy and dragged on intermittently from 1651 – 1674. The Dutch were the greatest naval power in Europe at the time. Again these wars had a direct impact upon Newfoundland. Dutch Admiral De Ruyter raided St. John's, Bay Bulls, and Petty Harbour in June 1665, ravaging shipping and shore equipment. Dutch privateers were an aggravation to trade and raided Ferryland in 1673, destroying cattle and burning fishing boats, devastating in terms of manpower, supplies and ship losses. These raids and the worry over the increase in French control on the south coast, raised the question of whether Newfoundland should be governed as a settled colony rather than just as a fishing base. This idea was against the West Country merchants' interests because it would mean the loss of their monopoly. As things stood, the merchants controlled the fishery and reaped the profits. Regulations in the Government Charters of 1661 and 1676 concerning Newfoundland stated that it was a naval recruiting ground and discouraged settlement. The English Board of Trade said in 1680 that "Newfoundland will always belong to the strongest-sea-power." The island was not self supporting, meaning settlers could not feed themselves or provide the clothing and necessities for survival – all supplies had to come by sea. Newfoundland existed by exporting its fish by ship. Therefore reality lay in this undisputable fact of possession by the strongest sea-power.

THE FISHING ADMIRALS

At this time, Newfoundland was governed by a system known as the "fishing admiralty," which lasted about 150 years. There was no resident year round governor in Newfoundland before 1729. The captain of the first ship to reach a harbour in the spring was the "admiral" of that harbour for the season and had the first choice of the fishing rooms; the second and third captains became the "vice" and "rear" admirals. The admiral and his assistants were responsible for administering justice. This system was not officially recognized by the British government until 1671. The system did not work well and lawlessness was rampant. Frequent complaints about the state of violence, anarchy and smuggling caused the British government to appoint the first governor with civil authority and the power to appoint magistrates who stayed on the island. The fishing admiral system declined within several years.

KING WILLIAM'S WAR

The War of the Spanish Succession, known in Newfoundland as King William's War, began in 1689 and lasted until 1697, posing many problems and creating a depression in the fishery. The Spanish and French markets were lost, enemies and pirates damaged the fleets and navy press gangs brought about a huge reduction in the number of men available for the fishery. England, Holland and Spain were fighting France. France had founded a colony at Placentia in 1662, and in 1696 the French led by d'Iberville raided the English colonies, destroying them, committing atrocities and acts of barbarism. In 1697 Newfoundland was in complete ruin and very few records of shipping, settlement and catches were kept during this period. The War of the Spanish Succession ended with the Treaty of Ryswick and military establishments with a garrison were set up by the British in Newfoundland by 1697.

QUEEN ANNE'S WAR

Newfoundland's English settlements were attacked on a regular basis by the French from Placentia during Queen Anne's War, 1702-1713. However, there was not much to destroy because the English had not had time to rebuild after the French offensive of 1696-97. The English wanted no further French settlement in Newfoundland. English settlers requested help from the foreign office to preserve the colony and protect it from the French.

The Treaty of Utrecht, marking the end of Queen Anne's War, acknowledged that Newfoundland belonged to Britain. The removal of the French settlers came about only because France had been defeated in land fighting in Europe and its royal and merchant navies destroyed. No further French settlement occured, but the French were permitted to catch fish and dry them on land from Cape Bonavista to Point Riche. The French fishery was monitored and supervised solely by English control, and this continued until 1783. The French were forbidden to stay during the winter or erect any kind of building, with the exception of the stages and huts needed for the drying of fish. This led to continuous disagreement between English and French fishermen and intermittent problems that have continued to the present time.

While war raged on, the fishery had to be carried out or it would never be renewed successfully in peacetime. The fishing merchant faced several problems in wartime: first, he had to get fishing ships, men and supplies to Newfoundland, then ensure a safe fishery there, and finally get the fish to market and the ships and men safely back to England at the end of the season. The growth of New England, which at this time still belonged to the English, made it easier to get supplies safely as ships sailed in waters dominated by the English.

THE SEVEN YEARS WAR

The Seven Years War (1756-1763) had a significant impact on trade. The British Empire became much larger, while the French lost their major possessions in North America. Britain's takeover of New France meant that ships from New France traded with England, not with France, and brought more passing shipping trade into Newfoundland waters. Planters and settlers found a greater opportunity to deal with traders and were not as dependent upon the West Country merchants as before. Population in Newfoundland increased after 1763 and there was also an increase in shipping and the amount of American trade to Newfoundland.

It was during this war that Newfoundland was invaded for the last time. The French arrived in Newfoundland and captured Bay Bulls on June 24, 1762. St. John's was difficult to attack by sea, so the French went overland and captured it on June 27. They sent a small detachment to Carbonear and Trinity and these settlements, except for Carbonear Island, were taken as well. St. John's was in the possession of the French from June 27 to September 20, 1762. Colonel Amherst, in charge of New World troops in New York, was notified of the problem and set out for St. John's. He captured Torbay and marched on to Signal Hill where a major battle took place. St. John's was retaken and the French left.

The British fishery began its last big phase of growth from 1763-70. There was a general expansion in business and an optimistic feeling as the French had been driven out of North America, except for St. Pierre and Miquelon. The French presence had been a dampening influence on English trade in Newfoundland and investment stymied with the threat of war at any time. The whole atmosphere changed after 1763. The fishing ship catch increased from 88,450 quintals in 1759 to 252,910 quintals in 1770. (A quintal, pronounced "kentall," is a hundred weight measure.)

The Treaty of Paris, after the Seven Years War, ceded French possessions in Canada to Britain. Labrador was removed from Quebec and attached to Newfoundland, thus our ownership of this vast tract of land originated in 1763, and the title recognized again in 1927 by His Majesty's Privy Council in England. French fishing rights in Newfoundland were finally verified along

"Petit Nord" from Cape Bonavista on the east coast to Pointe Riche on the western shore. The French were brought back to the south coast when the islands of St. Pierre and Miquelon were also given as a shelter for French fishermen on the Grand Banks. James Cook was appointed to do the surveys that would be needed in order to enforce these international agreements. St. Pierre and Miquelon were surveyed in 1763 before they were given to the French, then the French Shore and parts of the Labrador coasts were partially surveyed. James Cook's charts were remarkably accurate and strengthened Britain's expansion of the fishery into previously unexplored areas, helped the government curtail French demands for a larger share of the fishery and to keep them within their treaty limits.

While Hugh Palliser was Governor, from 1764-68, he charted the south coast near to the French islands and encouraged English settlement in this area. His main concern was to extend English fishing along the coasts and keep the French within the treaty limits. Palliser made an effort to increase fishing and sealing on the Labrador coast, creating a further demand for ships, fishermen and seamen. The migratory and sedentary fisheries grew and population rose on the island. However, the British government still sought to discourage settlement and to promote the migratory fishery.

England's preoccupation with the French Wars and the temporary restriction on French fishing had given an unanticipated help to settlement, and by the middle of the eighteenth century more than two thousand people were living in the area of St. John's. The second Act of Parliament concerning Newfoundland, called Palliser's Act, was passed in 1775. This Act was devised to deter English seamen from abandoning ship in

Newfoundland and as stated in a letter in the Colonial Office records, "To controvert the course of nature, to keep the island of Newfoundland a barren waste, to exterminate the inhabitants: to annihilate property, and to make sailors by preventing population." It began a renewal of hostility to settlers and was regarded with great hostility by the merchants.

THE AMERICAN WARS OF INDEPENDENCE

During the American Wars of Independence, 1775-1783, the navy was too busy with defense to pay much attention to settlement, and delayed enforcement of Palliser's Act. The supply routes between America and Newfoundland were cut, causing great but not lasting problems. The colonies in the United States, having gained their independence, were was no longer part of the British Empire, and were therefore unable to sell supplies to Newfoundland or the British West Indies. Newfoundland was forced to find other sources of food and lumber, and gradually replaced the American supply links by others in the Canadian Maritimes and Quebec. Newfoundland built its own ships and took over the West Indies fish markets. The migratory fishery had been destroyed during the war and the merchants had to rely more upon the inhabitant fishery for fish, inducing a large network of business enterprises to grow up around the Newfoundland coastline.

The Treaty of Versailles in 1783, gave France the islands of St. Pierre and Miquelon to "…prevent the quarrels between the two nations of England and France … take away the fishing rights between Cape Bonavista and Cape St. John and move it to the area between Cape John and Cape Ray on the west coast of the island." This treaty was also to Newfoundland's advantage as with the loss of their colony at Placentia the French could not attack overland in wartime as they had previously done. The French fishing fleet was working in unfriendly waters, making its fishery very difficult to operate. The French Shore was the cause of endless problems that continued to affect relations between Newfoundland and Britain for many years.

The years from 1783-1789 brought a great post war boom in settlement—the island's total population increased from about 10,000 to over 16,000 people. The boom collapsed in 1789, but the population did not decline. The Newfoundland population was now too large to remove from the island and could not be discouraged from growing. Numbers had dramatically increased and colonization was a fact. The British government was forced to abandon its policy of discouraging settlement.

War was indisputably the greatest factor after the fishery to determine Newfoundland's history. The Spanish and Portuguese fisheries declined because of long hard wars in Europe which destroyed vast numbers of ships and fishermen. Over the years the fishery was involved in warfare, diplomacy and peace negotiations. If the results of the Seven Years War and the American Revolutionary Wars had been different, the English position in Newfoundland would have been much weakened and England would not have been able to oppose the demands of the French, Spanish, or Americans for the supremacy of fishery and settlement in Newfoundland. The French defeated the British on the island, but, due to the outcome of the European Wars Newfoundland was ceded to the British with only fishing rights being given to the French. The French lost their Newfoundland colony and suffered a serious loss of capability to compete in the fishery. It was due to preoccupation with the wars in Europe that the British ignored the island for a time, enabling it to become settled to a point at which it could not be disregarded by Britain any longer – a colony in its own right.

EARLY GOVERNMENT

A resident governor was installed in Newfoundland by 1817 due to the increase in settlement and numbers of people involved in the fishery. Governors began to encourage agriculture, build roads and set up circuit courts.

Newfoundland received official colonial status in the mid 1820s. The settlers continuously pressed for participation in their local government and a representative assembly was granted in 1832. The traditional two house bi-cameral system of colonial government had a Crown appointed legislature and a 15 member representative assembly was elected from 9 districts. Difficulties finding a place for the assembly to sit brought about the construction of the Colonial Building, completed in 1850. Tensions between church and class divisions played a significant part in the islands political and social life. Demands continued to be made for responsible government.

Newfoundland received responsible government in 1855 and was then equal constitutionally to the other colonies in North America and elsewhere. Much of the money generated by good markets and prices in the fishery during the first years of responsible government was invested back into the island for public improvements and more business establishments. Newfoundland now had control over its economic life, but the economy was based on the fishery. Treaties in place giving privileges to France and the United States to fish, take bait and dry their fish on much of the island's coastline severely limited control of this fishery.

Newfoundland was plagued by many problems in this period when the government was attempting to diversify the economy away from total reliance on the fishery. A devastating cycle of depressions and recoveries began with huge amounts of relief being given to the people. A movement for Confederation with Canada began in the early 1860s but was defeated in 1869 and again in 1894. Railway construction to open up the island began in 1880, was held up by the contractors business failures, and were resumed again in 1890 by the Reid Newfoundland Company. Branch rail lines began to be constructed to the main towns in Conception Bay, Trinity and Bonavista Bays on the north east coast and to the mining industry that had developed in Notre Dame Bay. The Dry Dock was completed in St. John's in 1884 and brought more employment.

A financial crisis developed in 1894 when runs on Newfoundland's banks, due to reckless investment by officials, forced them to suspend payment. Newfoundland was in a serious position with an economy crippled by the resulting lack of capital and credit. Riots ensuing from the desperate financial distress of the people took place in St. John's. The Government of Britain helped with financial assistance and enabled the fishery to start up again.

The years up to 1914 were more prosperous for Newfoundland. In 1898 the government formed a contract with the Reid Newfoundland Company, selling them the railway, St. John's drydock, contracts for much of the coastal steamer service and the Gulf ferry and telegraph system, centralizing the railway in the west end of St. John's. The Royal Navy Reserve established a branch in St. John's in 1901. The iron ore mine at Bell Island was developed by the Nova Scotia Steel and Coal Company and the Dominion Iron and Steel Company, giving prosperity to the area and employment to hundreds of fishermen in the off season. The pulp and paper industry was introduced in 1905 with the opening of the Anglo Newfoundland Development Company in the Grand Falls area. The town of Grand Falls was built and a rail line constructed to the port of Botwood. A paper mill and the new town of Corner Brook were set up in 1923, and opened the west coast of the island to settlement. These new industries moved employment from complete reliance on the fishery. Newfoundland remained in a recovered atmosphere of activity in the pre World War I period.

WORLD WAR I

Newfoundland was a dominion of the British Empire in both world wars as it did not join Confederation with Canada until 1949. World War I was declared on August 28, 1914. Its historic **Royal Newfoundland Regiment** was re-activated—the first 500 volunteers were called the "Blue Puttees" due to their distinctive leggings—and fought against the Turks in Gallipoli and against the Germans in France. At the Battle of the Somme and Beaumont Hamel in France in 1916, Newfoundland suffered among the worst losses of any dominion. Nearly 4,000 Newfoundlanders are said to have been killed or wounded. Tommy Ricketts from Middle Arm, White Bay was awarded the Victoria Cross, the highest military award given in Britain, for bravery. Many others served in the British navy and in the Forestry Corps. Many women served as nurses in Canada, Britain and on the battlefields. At the end of the war the New-

Man of War vessels in St. John's harbour, circa 1886

foundland people bought 100 acres of the battlefield at Beaumont Hamel and dedicated it to the memory of the brave men who served in the regiment. A bronze Caribou, the exact replica of which stands in Bowring Park in St. John's, overlooks Newfoundland Park at Beaumont Hamel. Memorial University and the War Memorial are tributes to the veterans and the war dead. Newfoundland's war effort and contribution caused it to come out of the war with a debt of over $19,000,000.

COMMISSION OF GOVERNMENT

The depression in the 1930s, combined with the huge debt incurred in World War I, brought hard times to Newfoundland. Frustration and unemployment led rioting crowds to attack the assembly in 1932. The financial position became critical and Britain took over responsibility for Newfoundland's debts with the appointment of the Commission of Government. The Commission, composed of the governor and six commissioners -three British civil servants and three Newfoundlanders- replaced the legislature in February 1934. The Commission was intended to be temporary, but continued when World War II broke out.

WORLD WAR II

Newfoundland, located strategically at the eastern edge of North America, was called a "floating fortress in the Atlantic" in World War II, and was thus of enormous importance. Its men served in the British and Canadian forces – 3,419 in the Royal Navy, 3,056 in the Royal Artillery and the R.A.F., 600 in the Canadian services, and hundreds in the Merchant Navy. More than 500 women were WRENS, CWACS or WAAFS. One of the largest airfields in the world was located in Gander in 1939 at the beginning of the war, and Newfoundland was a starting and refuelling point on the way to Europe.

The sea lanes were kept open for supplies without which victory might have gone to the other side. Over a thousand merchant ships had been lost in 1942. Convoys gathered in St. John's harbour to be escorted by an all Canadian escort group, before setting off to Europe. One of these, in 1944, was the largest in history – 167 ships. These convoys faced the threat of mines and torpedoes from the waiting German U-boats patrolling in Newfoundland and Atlantic waters.

Mines were set outside the harbour, but were cleared by mine-sweepers. Torpedoes exploded into the chain boom and metal mesh anti-submarine nets across St. John's Narrows in March 1942, but did no damage. Two loaded iron ore carriers

Courtesy PANL

Submarine in St. John's harbour, WWII

were torpedoed and sunk at Wabana, Bell Island in Conception Bay. In 1941 Roosevelt and Churchill signed the famous Atlantic Charter in Placentia Bay near Argentia which declared "All men in all lands may live out their lives in freedom from fear and want."

American bases were built in Newfoundland in 1941 under the 1940 Destroyers for Bases deal. The arrival of the Americans brought vast changes to Newfoundland and Labrador and well-paid jobs became available. Newfoundland, prior to WWII, was a society of native-born people. It was a radically different place after people from the U.S., Canada and other places around the world arrived here with the armed forces. Fort Pepperrell became the headquarters of the U.S. Northeast Air Command and one of the NATO bases. St. John's harbour was used by the Royal Navy, the Royal Canadian Navy and the United States Navy.

Canada also established significant military facilities – a naval base, two hospitals, a naval barracks at Buckmaster's Circle, a military barracks at Lester's Field and an airport at Torbay. All these brought about virtually full employment, more money in circulation, and prosperity.

CONFEDERATION

The British government did not want to carry on the Commission of government indefinitely and a time for change came in 1945, when Newfoundland was financially self supporting. The debate resumed on return to responsible government. The constitutional position had to be settled first as there was no established procedure to give Newfoundland back its government.

The British government set up a National Convention in Newfoundland to examine its financial and economic conditions and make recommendations on the forms of future government to be placed on the referendum ballot. Delegates from every Newfoundland and Labrador district met in the Colonial Building. The Convention recommended on the ballot the two options of either continued Commission of government or return to responsible government. Canada recognised through its wartime experience the strategic importance of maintaining a foothold in Newfoundland and was also concerned about the continued presence of the Americans on the island. Confederation with Canada was not recommended on the ballot. but. the British government decided to include it as a third option in the referendum. Two referenda were held and in the second, on July 22, 1948, Confederation with Canada won with a very close majority of 52%. A seven man delegation was chosen to debate the terms of union signed with Canada on December 11, 1948. Newfoundland became the tenth province of Canada on March 31, 1949.

It was said that Newfoundland joined Confederation "Not by bullets but by ballots."

With the introduction of Confederation six Newfoundlanders were appointed to the Senate, seven federal members of Parliament were elected to go to Ottawa and Joseph Smallwood became the first premier of the province of Newfoundland and Labrador. Confederation brought social changes in the form of Unemployment Insurance, Old Age Pensions, government paid medical care and hospitals and increased payments for education.

CHAPTER TWO

Forts of Old St. John's

Historically, fortifications were built in St. John's to provide a safe harbour and refuge from attack for fishermen, rather than for the defense of the town or people. 173 years of British military presence in Newfoundland began in 1697 when the British fortified the port. There were seven active batteries during the 1700s and 1800s. Later, after Newfoundland became a colony, the fortifications were used for the protection of the town, which had become the trading and recreation centre of the island. Fortifications developed as did technology. All were at sea level at first with the cannons at the narrowest point of the harbour entrance. Eventually, fortifications were moved to Fort William in the east end of the town, then to Fort Frederick and later to Fort Townshend on the higher levels.

FORT WILLIAM

This fort was an important part of St. John's for over two hundred years. It was built in 1680 to defend against continuous attacks by pirates and privateers. The British were reluctant to build fortifications in Newfoundland, but the fort was improved in 1771 and again in 1795 and was the principal defense for the town and harbour for most of the 18th century. The barracks for the imperial garrison stationed at Fort William

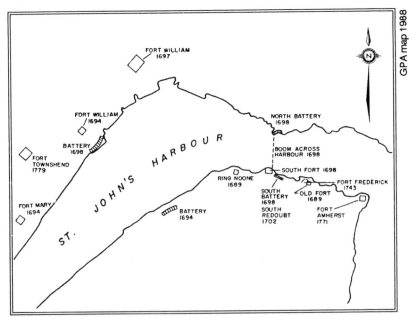

Three centuries of St. John's harbour fortifications.

remained until 1871. Fort William then served as a railway station until the completion of the new station on Water Street in 1903. In 1953 a plaque commemorating the old fort was placed at the Newfoundland Hotel which had been built on the site where the fort once stood.

FREDERICK'S BATTERY

Frederick's Battery is located between Fort Amherst and Prosser's Rock, the area of the new small boat basin. A battery was established in 1665 after the Dutch Admiral De Ruyter attacked the city. This was rebuilt in 1776 and named Frederick's Battery. Local landowners have recently refused permission for an archaeological dig in the area because of trespassing and parking problems. There can be no development in the area without resolution of this issue. A pile of rocks from the old fortifications can be seen and many artifacts have been found on the site.

FORT TOWNSHEND

This large fortification was built in 1779 to house the military. Its location, just west of the Basilica of St. John the Baptist, was a better site from which to view the harbour and fire upon whoever was in control of Signal Hill than was Fort William. The military withdrew from St. John's in 1870 and most of the fortifications were levelled and allowed to fall into disrepair. The former site of Fort Townshend is the present location of the Royal Newfoundland Constabulary and the Central Fire Station.

FORT AMHERST

Located on the opposite side of the Narrows from Signal Hill, Fort Amherst held a defense position for over 400 years. In 1762 the British tried to stop invasions of St. John's by extending a chain from Chain Rock to Pancake Rock, and in 1777 constructed the fort. A stone lighthouse was built on the site in 1813. All has now fallen into ruin except the lighthouse and fog horn. The fort was reactivated for defense in both World Wars. In World War II a submarine net was placed between Chain and Pancake Rocks to prevent attacks against the harbour by German U-boats, often seen outside the harbour entrance. The fortifications and guns can still be seen at Fort Amherst, as well as a small new lighthouse and foghorn constructed in 1954 to aid navigation.

OLD ST JOHN'S — THE DOWNTOWN CORE

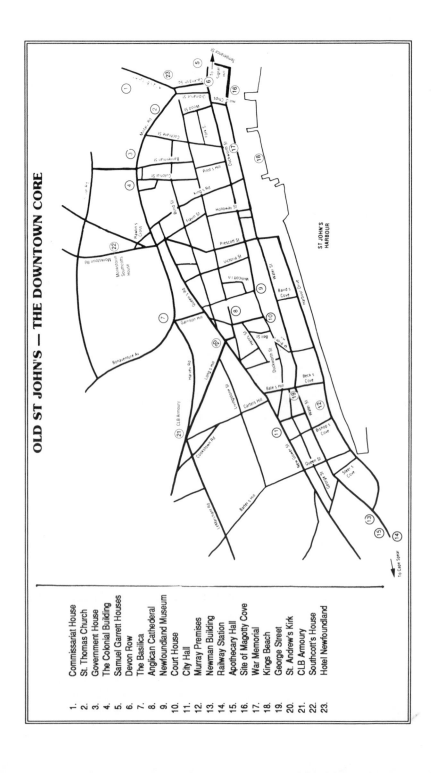

1. Commissariat House
2. St. Thomas Church
3. Government House
4. The Colonial Building
5. Samuel Garrett Houses
6. Devon Row
7. The Basilica
8. Anglican Cathedral
9. Newfoundland Museum
10. Court House
11. City Hall
12. Murray Premises
13. Newman Building
14. Railway Station
15. Apothecary Hall
16. Site of Magotty Cove
17. War Memorial
18. Kings Beach
19. George Street
20. St. Andrew's Kirk
21. CLB Armoury
22. Southcott's House
23. Hotel Newfoundland

ST JOHN'S HARBOUR

To Cape Spear

Excavation at South Castle

SOUTH CASTLE BATTERY

Throughout the history of St. John's harbour, Chain Rock on the east side and Anchor Point on the west side of the narrows were heavily fortified. These batteries worked with Fort William to defend the harbour. The site of South Castle is fenced off near Prosser's Rock small boat basin. Gerald Penney, an archaeologist, investigated the site in 1988 as part of an environmental study on the Prosser's Rock small boat basin. He said that South Castle was called a "pretty little castle all of stone and substantial timber" by contemporary observer Reverend John Jackson in 1706, and that castle was a common English term for seacoast defenses which contained a tower or "keep." The battery was called South Battery and South Redoubt by its builder, Captain Michael Richards. The substantial eight gun battery and ancillary fort was built at Anchor Point between 1700 and 1703. It withstood French takeover in the winter of

1703 for 33 days but was taken by land and destroyed by St. Ovide in January 1709. The battery was believed to be 120 feet long and about 15 feet high. It may have had a wooden sentry and signalling tower, a guardhouse and a powder magazine. The effect of the design was to provide fire like a ship's broadside, to attack an enemy ship attempting to enter the harbour. The battery was thought to have replaced an even older earthworks battery right on top of Anchor Point. More than 5,000 glass, ceramic and metal artifacts were recovered in 1988 and are held at the Newfoundland Museum. The derrick pad for World War II submarine nets has been excavated at the South Castle dig.

FORT WALDEGRAVE (North Castle Battery)
Constructed in 1798 as a temporary battery on the site of the old North Castle Battery above Chain Rock, Fort Waldegrave was used until the 1860s. The battery was reused during World War I with gun placements constructed to protect the Narrows. The gun area is presently a parking lot overlooking the Narrows and the placements can still be seen.

QUEENS BATTERY
For centuries France and England vied for possession of St. John's and in 1762 British and French forces fought the last North American battle of the Seven Years War on the slopes of Signal Hill. The fortifications date from the 1840s and 1850s. The barracks and the gun placements have been reconstructed at the original site on Signal Hill below Cabot Tower. The *Signal Hill Tattoo*, a reenactment of a battle scene between the British and French in authentic period uniform, can be seen and heard near the *Queens Battery* each day during July and August.

St. John's Harbour from near Fort Amherst, circa 1886

CUCKOLD'S COVE AND QUIDI VIDI

Batteries were set up at Cuckold's Cove and Quidi Vidi to prevent enemy landings that might take the town from these positions. Legend has it that Cuckold's Cove got its name from a dual fought there between two officers of the old garrison on Signal Hill. It was said that one officer accused the other of paying undue attention to his wife. So, the "Cuckolded" officer challenged the other to a duel. Unfortunately, however, it seems that in this case justice did not triumph - the aggrieved party was killed and his fellow officer proceeded to marry the widow!

The narrow entrance to Quidi Vidi, known as the Gut, is a short distance along the shoreline from Cuckold's Cove. Quidi Vidi Village is a small picturesque fishing village, with old houses, wharves and small boats. Above the entrance to the small harbour is the Quidi Vidi Battery, a reconstructed French fortification from the French capture of St. John's in 1762. The British rebuilt and occupied the fort in 1780 until they left Newfoundland in 1870. The battery was restored as a Centennial project in 1967 from old plans and archaeological data.

FORT PEPPERRELL

This US military base was located between Quidi Vidi and the White Hills. The US was granted land in 1941 on a free 99 year lease to construct naval and air bases for the eventuality of attack by Germany. The construction brought millions of dollars into the local economy, an enormous boost after the depression years. Newfoundland entered a period of unprecedented prosperity. The coming of the Cold War meant the building of early warning radar sites in northern Labrador and the continued presence of the Americans. It is estimated that during these years 25,000 Newfoundland women married U.S. personnel. The Americans also built the first modern pier in the port. The pier was in use until 1961 when it was taken over by the National Harbours Board of Canada. The US moved out of Newfoundland in 1966 and turned the Fort Pepperrell base, now known as Pleasantville, back to the province. The base hospital was reopened as the Dr. Charles A. Janeway Hospital for Sick Children. The Canadian military, Canadian Forces Base Pleasantville, is located on part of the former U.S. base.

ST JOHN'S: THE NEW EXTENDED CITY

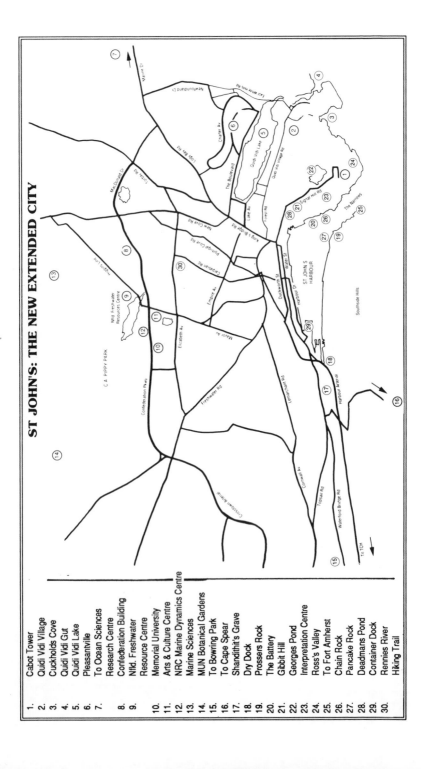

1. Cabot Tower
2. Quidi Vidi Village
3. Cuckholds Cove
4. Quidi Vidi Gut
5. Quidi Vidi Lake
6. Pleasantville
7. To Ocean Sciences Research Centre
8. Confederation Building
9. Nfld. Freshwater Resource Centre
10. Memorial University
11. Arts & Culture Centre
12. NRC Marine Dynamics Centre
13. Marine Sciences
14. MUN Botanical Gardens
15. To Bowring Park
16. To Cape Spear
17. Shandithi's Grave
18. Dry Dock
19. Prossers Rock
20. The Battery
21. Gibbit Hill
22. Georges Pond
23. Interpretation Centre
24. Ross's Valley
25. To Fort Amherst
26. Chain Rock
27. Pancake Rock
28. Deadmans Pond
29. Container Dock
30. Rennies River Hiking Trail

CHAPTER THREE

Landmarks and Historic Sites of St. John's

St. JOHN'S has had a long and colourful history as the oldest port city on the North American continent. The entrance into St. John's harbour consists of a narrow gap leading into a deep bay. Because of its harbour and proximity to the fishing grounds, St. John's became a commercial trading outpost for the Basques, French, Spanish, Portuguese and English engaged in the fishery. The harbour was used as a meeting place for fishermen, with Portuguese and Spanish trawlers frequent visitors from about 1627 until more recent years. The city grew around its perfectly landlocked harbour – a haven from storms. Only in the last century did St. John's take on the appearance of a town. In 1810 it consisted of one narrow street with batteries and fortifications on the higher area of the town. Today it is a thriving city that has spread to the north and west of the original town. There are many quaint fishing villages close to St. John's and coastal scenery to view within a half hour drive. Sailing in and out of the Narrows on a boat tour is an experience you won't forget. The view of the city from the southside of the harbour is spectacular.

St. John's has been a centre of Newfoundland life with shipping connections to the U.S., Britain, and Canada. It has been a place for the distribution of goods and base for the fishing fleets. It served as a naval base in the War of 1812 and in the two world wars. Today, many buildings and historic sites stand as landmarks to the rich history of St. John's and its harbour.

The very fabric and structure of the city of St. John's reflects its political history. Many of its streets are named for former governors -- Gower, Prescott, Bannerman. Cochrane; or for people significant in its growth. Growth of the town was slow until the 19th century when big houses and urban wealth in the town core around the Colonial Building and Government House reflected its importance as an economic, administrative, religious and educational centre of the island.

There was no town council until 1888. Most of the best land in the town was owned by absentee landlords who strongly opposed municipal taxation. The government held the reins of most of the institutions and services of St. John's until that time.

Railway centralization at the end of the 19th century in the west end of the town reinforced its importance as an economic centre. The town boundaries until about the 1940s had been inside the old track on Empire Avenue. Town planning began during the time of the Commission of Government with the formation of the St. John's Housing Corporation. The town as it grew began to spread from its urban downtown core to the north and west.

Confederation with Canada brought federal funding for buildings such as the Sir Humphrey Gilbert Building on Duck-worth Street, the Post Office on Water Street and St. John's Harbour redevelopment. Hotel Newfoundland and the New-foundland Dockyard were taken over by Canadian National, a government Crown corporation. Joseph Smallwood built a new

Confederation Building for other provincial legislature and government offices on Prince Philip Drive and Memorial University built a new larger campus on Elizabeth Avenue.

The St. John's Waterfront is a popular place for both visitors and locals to drive and walk, to see and hear the activity of the many ships in for supplies, repairs or to deliver cargo. The downtown is still the heart of the city with its old buildings and harbourfront. It has become a tradition on New Year's Eve to visit the "waterfront" and bring in the New Year with thousands of merrymakers enjoying the festivities, fireworks and ship's whistles at midnight.

ST. JOHN'S FIRES

St. John's had three major fires in the 1800s – 1816, 1846 and the devastating 1892 fire. Most houses in St. John's were built entirely of wood and irregularly huddled together. Over 11,000 people were left homeless in the 1892 fire with 1572 houses burnt to the ground. All left standing in most of the downtown area were chimneys and the great empty walls of churches and larger stone buildings. Most of the downtown area within the Cookstown Road, Carter's Hill, and Beck's Cove in the west and Harvey Road and Military Road in the north burned in the fire. The property damage was estimated at $20,000,000 with less than $5,000,000 covered by insurance. Most of the main shops, warehouses and business and professional areas were completely gutted and the main public buildings, the hospital, the Anglican Cathedral and many churches also lay in ruins. The town rebuilt and recovered with the help of many supporters and benefactors.

Each of these fires brought about improvements and chan-

Courtesy PANL

St. John's after the Great Fire of 1892

ges. Streets were straightened and widened, there were new layouts, rebuilding, and firebreaks made – some of which have become well known streets today. The Roman Catholic and Anglican churches were built in this period. St. Andrew's Presbyterian church, the Congregational church and new Colonial Building were also completed. The fires had an influence on building materials and the merchants began to build in brick or stone.

Another devastating fire occurred in December of 1942 when the Knights of Columbus Hostel on Harvey Road caught fire during a Saturday night dance for servicemen. 99 people were killed and 107 injured. There are theories that the fire may have been the result of enemy sabotage. Ironically, another major fire hit the same spot exactly 50 years later, in December 1992. The CLB Armoury and the area on LeMarchant Road and

Long's Hill were gutted, but no lives were lost in the 1992 fire. High winds and intense heat caused the fire to almost become out of control.

DOWNTOWN ST. JOHN'S

The main downtown street, Water Street, was in the city's early days nothing more than a row of fish flakes. It was called the Lower Path, and quickly became the centre of city life and commerce. The premises of all the merchants were located along its length. The names of Bowring, Ayre, Macpherson, Knowling, Devine, Newman, Milley, Wood, Outerbridge, Harvey, Murray, Job, Martin, Royal, Hutton, Steers, Hickman, Pratt, Clouston, Dicks and many others were prominent in the town's trade and business. Most of the stores had several wharves, fish stores or warehouses built on the north side of the harbour. The street was once paved with cobblestones while the other streets were hard packed dirt.

Water Street has undergone significant changes caused by fire and reconstruction over the years and new heritage by-laws have guaranteed that no longer will old buildings of character be allowed to be destroyed. The exteriors of many are being restored and the interiors modified for contemporary use. Yellowbelly Corner at Water Street and Beck's Cove is but one example of the past style of building on this historic street. Today the old brick and stone buildings still give the street an old world charm. You can enjoy a leisurely stroll along its length and enjoy the sights and sounds of the harbour. Water Street is the heart of downtown.

Street cars on tracks were once a familiar sight in the downtown area, running along Water Street, Duckworth Street, past the Newfoundland Hotel, up Military Road to Rawlins Cross, down Queen's Road to Adelaide Street and back to Water Street. The street cars ran from the turn of the century until they were replaced by buses in 1948.

Duckworth Street was called the Upper Path when there were only two major roadways in St. John's. Now a busy commercial centre, one of the oldest streets in the city has had many homes converted to offices, delightful shops and restaurants – a blend of traditional and contemporary businesses. Its heritage can be seen in the many historic buildings along its length.

Today, St. John's has the most pubs per capita in Canada, many of which are located on George Street. One can walk up and down, dropping into the numerous restaurants, night clubs and taverns, enjoying the atmosphere and considerable choice of music. There is something for everybody – blues. jazz, western, alternate, rock, contemporary or traditional Newfoundland music. Thousands are drawn to the open air concerts, festivals and social events in the summertime. George Street is one of the main attractions of the city!

Courtesy PANL VA69 11-1

Water Street, St. John's circa1886

HISTORIC BUILDINGS

ARCHITECTURE

St. John's is a city with fine examples of architecture and many brightly painted wooden houses. Despite the destruction wrought by the fires, many buildings standing today show our past and are preserved by heritage by-laws.

Southcott style of architecture. The firm of J. and J.T. Southcott are said to have come from England in the mid 1800s to build houses for the Cable Company in Heart's Content. J.T. Southcott, the first trained architect in Newfoundland, introduced the *Mansard* roof to St. John's. The Southcott Style is *Second Empire*, typified by a concave shaped mansard roof with rounded bonnet shape dormer windows, and bay windows on the ground

J.T. Southcott's home (28 Monkstown Road) was at one time operated as a hospital by Mary Southcott.

floor. It was mainly built in the period from 1870-1900. The Southcott style became the most representative of St. John's architecture during the time when most of the city had to be rebuilt after the 1892 fire. Southcott's own house at 28 Monkstown Road, built in 1875, survived the 1892 fire and typifies this type of design. Southcott's daughter Mary lived in this house and operated a small private hospital there in 1918 for maternity, women and children.

Victorian Gothic is represented by a saddle roofed building with a steep pitch, decorated with Gothic revival details and built in the period between 1840-1900.

Queen Anne style houses are usually imposing in size, using many roof forms and details such as decorative shingling and applications from other styles. This style of house was built in the period between 1905-1915.

A common form of architecture used in St. John's, the bracketed style is comprised of a flat roofed building with brackets under the eaves.

Among the distinctive architecture of downtown St. John's houses are the five houses located on Devon Row, near Hotel Newfoundland, which survived the fire of 1892. They were constructed by James J. Southcott in the Second Empire Style in about 1870-1877. A row of four Second Empire stone houses on Temperance Street, a little east of Devon Row, were built for his four daughters by Samuel Garret, the stone mason who built Cabot Tower. They were built entirely of the unused stone from Cabot Tower during the times when the weather was too bad to work on the top of Signal Hill. The houses are four storeys at the back and three at the front.

Yellowbelly Corner, the area at Becks Cove at Water Street,

was a meeting place for Irishmen from Wexford, who wore yellow sashes or badges. The brick and stone buildings are classical commercial vernacular constructed about 1840-60.

THE ROMAN CATHOLIC BASILICA

The Basilica, located on Military Road, was designed by John Jones of Ireland in the Romanesque style. It was built of limestone and granite in the form of a Latin cross with two forty-two metre (138 ft.) high twin towers at the front. The sandstone was quarried in Kelly's Island, Conception Bay, Newfoundland; the limestone came from Ireland, and Dublin granite was used to face the windows and quoins. The building took fourteen years to complete and was consecrated in 1855. It was begun by Bishop Fleming who wanted to build a symbol of the Catholic Church and its importance in the social, economic and political life of St. John's. At the time of its completion the Roman Catholic Cathedral of St. John the Baptist was the largest church in the north of the New World. It was the only principal church in the city to survive the 1892 fire undamaged.

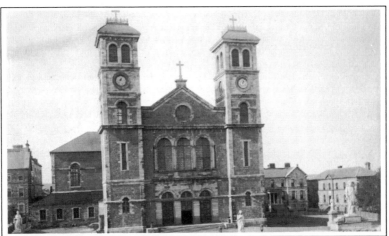

Courtesy PANL VA69 4-1

The Basilica of St. John the Baptist, circa 1886

The church was raised to the rank of minor Basilica in 1955 on its centenary. At that time, several thousand Portuguese fishermen paraded to the church to donate the statue of *Our Lady of Fatima*. The event celebrated the special relationship that had long existed between Newfoundland and the Portuguese fishermen who for many years came to St. John's harbour with the famous "White Fleet." The Basilica has been designated a National Historic Site. It has some excellent statuary and a beautiful intricately painted ceiling highlighted in gold leaf. It is one of the best known landmarks of the city and affords an excellent view of the harbour and downtown area from its front steps.

ANGLICAN CATHEDRAL

The Cathedral is the oldest Anglican parish in North America. Construction began in 1847, of white sandstone from Scotland and bluestone quarried in the Southside Hills. The Cathedral is said to be the finest example of ecclesiastical Neo Gothic architecture in North America, and was designed by Sir George Gilbert Scott. The nave functioned as the church until the transepts and Choir were completed in 1885. The design is of a Latin Cross with characteristic Gothic discordant parts and asymmetry of carving, stonework and design. The Cathedral was given an official coat of arms when it became elevated to Diocese status in 1839. Newfoundland now has three Dioceses, with the Cathedral representing Eastern Newfoundland and Labrador.

The Cathedral was destroyed in the fire of 1892 and left a shell. The interior was rebuilt within the remaining exterior walls a few years later. The nave and aisles are excellent ex-

The Anglican Cathedral

amples of Gothic Revival. Many magnificent carvings, gargoyles, stained glass windows (one of which escaped the fire), a reredos (ornamental screen of carved white freestone behind the altar designed by Giles Gilbert Scott), and beautifully designed woodwork are to be found inside this Cathedral on Church Hill. A small church museum is open to the public during guided tours.

The Anglican Cathedral was designated a National Historic Site on June 19, 1981 and is a must for those interested in church architecture.

ST. ANDREW'S PRESBYTERIAN KIRK

The Kirk is constructed of Accrington brick and finished in Scottish freestone. It is said to be one of the finest examples of serence architecture amongst the city's churches and is located on the corner of Long's Hill and Queens Road.

GOWER STREET UNITED CHURCH
Once called "The Cathedral of Newfoundland Methodism," this Romanesque red brick building stands just across from the Anglican Cathederal, at the top of Church Hill.

ST. THOMAS' CHURCH

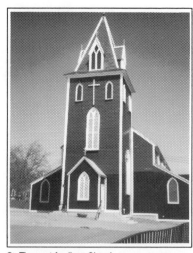

The oldest standing church in St. John's, St. Thomas', opened in 1836 and was the official church of the Newfoundland Garrison until they withdrew in 1871. The church was moved six inches from its foundations in the Great Gale of 1846. Wings were then added on the north and south sides to secure the building. Many houses near the "Old

St. Thomas' Anglican Church

Garrison Church" were constructed in Second Empire style and most of that area on Military Road survived the fire of 1892.

COMMISSARIAT HOUSE
Commissariat House was constructed in 1818-19 to serve as the offices and residence of the Assistant Commissary General, located on King's Bridge Road near the Old Garrison Church. It served a function in the supply of provisions and services to the British military in St. John's. The Georgian style building has been restored and furnished in the 1830 period, and is open to the public in the summer with interpretive guides dressed in period costume.

GOVERNMENT HOUSE

Government House on Military Road was built by Governor Sir Thomas Cochrane, as a residence for the governors of Newfoundland. Constructed of local red sandstone trimmed with English Portland stone, it was begun in 1827, and took five years to complete, costing three times the original estimate. The two story building consists of a centre block flanked by slightly lower wings on the east and west. The ceilings in its reception room and ball rooms were beautifully painted by a Polish prisoner, Alexander Pindikowski, who also painted frescos on ceilings in the Colonial Building and Presentation Convent. His sentence was shortened by one month for his good work. Spacious grounds surround this sombre residence, one of the few buildings in North America surrounded by a twelve foot deep dry moat. The building is still used as the private residence of the Lieutenant Governor of Newfoundland and Labrador.

Sketch of Government House by H.B. Goodridge

COLONIAL BUILDING

Built of limestone in the Classical Revival style with massive Ionic columns, the Colonial Building was completed in 1850. It was built to house the Legislature of Newfoundland, and government offices from 1850-1960. The Provincial Archives are presently located in this imposing building on Military Road near Bannerman Park.

The Colonial Building

CONFEDERATION BUILDING

The Provincial House of Assembly was transferred from the Colonial Building to the new Confederation building on Prince Philip Drive in 1960. The building houses government offices and a new annex was completed in 1986. The grounds contain statues of John Cabot, Sir Wilfrid Grenfell, Gaspar Corte Real, a monument to the Ocean Ranger — a disaster in which an oil rig went down in a storm on 15 February 1982 with a loss of eighty-four lives, and a totem pole carved by a British Columbian Indian.

As with the statue of our Lady of Fatima at the Basilica, the statue of Corte Real is an indication of the long-standing friendship between Newfoundland and Portugal. In 1965 the bronze statue of the explorer, who visited Labrador in 1500-02, was donated to the Government of Newfoundland and Labrador by the Portuguese government and placed in position in front of the Confederation Building overlooking the harbour. The inscription reads:

> Gaspar Corte Real, Portuguese Navigator. He reached Terra Nova in the 15th century at the beginning of an era of great discoveries. From the Portuguese Fisheries Organization as an expression of gratitude on the behalf of the Portuguese Grand Banks fishermen for the friendly hospitality always extended to them by the people of Terra Nova – May 1965.

THE COURTHOUSE

The Court House was built on the original site of the custom's building which was produce market, post office and public gallows. The cornerstone was laid in 1901 by the Duke and Duchess of Cornwall. Completed in 1904, the Courthouse was constructed of red granite from the Southside Hills in Neo Romanesque style. This im-

The old custom's house, site of today's Court House

posing building, located on Water and Duckworth Streets, was once used as offices for the Colonial Secretary, the Cabinet and

Prime Ministers of Newfoundland. The Court House is now used for judicial purposes and because of its style and age has been named a National Historic Site.

THE MURRAY PREMISES
Previously one of the oldest warehouses on the harbourfront, these lovely renovated white stone buildings now house specialty shops, a pub and offices. The Murray Premises were built in the 1840s and escaped the fire of 1892. They are now a National Historic Site.

NEWFOUNDLAND MUSEUM
The Newfoundland Museum, designed by an English architect, was rebuilt from the Athenaeum building that was destroyed in the 1892 fire. The museum on Duckworth Street, opened in 1907, contains artifacts of the Beothuk Indians, also relics from early colonies and many paintings of Newfoundland's history. The Museum contains native peoples, european settlement and natural history exhibits on its three floors.

CITY HALL
The new City Hall on New Gower Street was officially opened in 1970. It has been called the best modern building in St. John's, and houses the Council chambers, Mayors office, municipal offices, city archives, a library and Tourist Information centre. Mile 0 of the Trans-Canada highway is located in front of City Hall on New Gower Street and is a popular spot for photographs. Terry Fox began his cross Canada run from this spot.

MEMORIAL UNIVERSITY COMPLEX

The old Memorial University College was located on the site of the Fort Townshend Parade Grounds on Parade Street. It was opened in 1925 with a student population of 55. The college was established as a memorial to Newfoundland's war dead and veterans of the First World War and later encompassed those of the Second World War. The college was admitted to university status in 1949. The university moved to its new campus on Elizabeth Avenue and Prince Philip Drive in 1961.

Memorial has grown rapidly. The university has six Faculties: Arts, Science, Education, Medicine, Engineering and Business Administration; and seven Schools – Graduate Studies, Nursing, Physical Education and Athletics, Social Work, Continuing Studies, Music and Pharmacy. It also offers degree programs in Fine Arts. There are now approximately 20,000 full and part-time students in Memorial's faculties and professional schools. The university library holds in excess of three million volumes on its shelves. Researchers in St. John's and around the world avail of the library's branches – the main Queen Elizabeth II Library, the Health Sciences Library and the Marine Institute Library. The Queen Elizabeth II Library houses the Centre for Newfoundland Studies.

The St. John's Campus covers approximately 220 acres. Many special divisions have been established over the years to meet the expanding needs of the province. As well the Marine Sciences Research Laboratory in Logy Bay, The National Research Council's Institute for Marine Dynamics – The Centre for Cold Ocean Resources Engineering are affiliated with Memorial. The Marine Institute – offering courses and programs in Marine and Fisheries technology, is also now affiliated with the university. A campus was established in Corner Brook in 1975 and was subsequently named Sir Wilfred Grenfell College. Memorial also established a small residential campus in Harlow, England. It provides accommodation for students and academic staff while they gain field experience in the United Kingdom and also acts as a base for teaching credit courses.

THE PORT OF ST. JOHN'S

St. John's harbour is formed of a bay one and one-half miles long and up to half a mile wide, with a narrow shallow entrance leading to the Atlantic Ocean. The 500-600 foot high cliffs protect the harbour from the Atlantic gales. The narrow entrance prevents large waves from penetrating the harbour and it is only during easterly storms that part of the harbour is somewhat affected. The waves usually break between Chain Rock and Pancake Rock, where the entrance is narrowest. The city is located on the north shore of the bay. The harbour has a tidal range of two to four feet, with a depth of twenty-six to thirty feet at its thirty-seven berths. There are over three miles of berths around the harbour, with four berths for refuelling.

Courtesy PANL

St. John's harbour in the days of sail

St. John's Harbour, circa 1886

Throughout Newfoundland's history, the port had a role as service station of the North Atlantic. Fishing ships and fleets took on water, fuel, food and provisions. Fishing ships used the port for recreation for their crews. Repairs were done in port at the dry dock at the west end of the harbour. The harbour was a natural protection from the North Atlantic gales.

Before the days of the auxiliary engine, dories rowed by oarsmen towed schooners into St. John's harbour. Schooners anchored or tied up to the many wharves with their sails drying in the sun would be a typical scene in the harbour. It was said that one could almost walk across the harbour on the decks of schooners anchored there. Cargo was loaded and unloaded by stevedores. In the winter the harbour would sometimes freeze over and ships froze into the ice. The port was one of great importance to the allies in World War I and II, supplying convoys on their transatlantic crossings. The guns at Fort Amherst and the attachments for the submarine nets across the mouth of the harbour are lasting testimonials of this.

HARBOUR PILOTS
When a ship nears port it radios its port agent informing the

Dories towing sailboat in St. John's harbour

The distribution of dried fish on the quay at St. Nalo after the fushing season. Steel engraving from *The Graphic*, October 17, 1891.

time of arrival. The agent then contacts the harbour master who assigns a berth, informs the Coast Guard traffic manager and dispatches a pilot boat. The pilot tug guides the ship to its berth. The pilot boat must be used by all foreign, and most large local ships.

HARBOUR RECONSTRUCTION IN THE 50s

In 1956, the federal department of public works began a study to modernize the harbour. The port of St. John's had been prevented from efficient and economic operation for many reasons. For years progress of industry and business on the Avalon peninsula was adversely affected by the absence of overall planning and co-ordination of harbour developments, crowding and inadequacy of existing wharf facilities and lack of mechanical equipment. The harbour of St. John's became unable to compete with Halifax and Montreal in freight handling in the new age of mass production and bigger ships. The roads around the old harbour had been built for horses and not large trucks.

Access to the southside and a new general cargo pier in the west end, with direct access to rail service were begun. Homes were removed from the southside, and a quarry started from which one million tons of fill was used for the new work in 1965. The harbour was dredged, marginal wharves replaced old finger-piers, a small boat basin developed, new wharves built for the Department of Transport, Canadian Coast Guard Regional Supply Base and a four lane service road built on the north side. Twenty million dollars was spent to ensure the controlled flow of traffic necessary for a modern harbour. The harbour sewage system was also modernized, and new pipes laid to the fuel storage tanks on the southside hill.

St. John's is now a modern year-round port catering to ships from around the world. The most frequent cargo to the port is fuel, which is loaded unto smaller ships or trucks for distribution. The port brings about $150 million of business to St. John's each year. The 200 mile limit for the fishery has placed fishery patrol boats in the port. Containerized cargo is now the principal means of transport with twice weekly shipping runs from St. John's to Halifax, Montreal and Saint John, N.B.

THE NEWFOUNDLAND DOCKYARD

St. John's was always a centre of repair for seagoing vessels. Two million dollars was spent to modernize the dry dock in the 1920s. During World War II the Newfoundland Dockyard worked around the clock to repair damaged ships. The

Courtesy PANL

St. John's Dockyard, circa 1895

Drydock can handle ships up to 170 metres long for repair. A new syncrolift has been installed on the area next to the drydock, lifting much larger ships out of the water for repair on the ground level. This provides an interesting view, for those interested in boats, on the drive to Fort Amherst on the Southside of the harbour.

AREAS OF INTEREST
AROUND THE HARBOUR & ST. JOHN'S

SIGNAL HILL—The 500 foot high hill overlooking the Narrows was used for almost 300 years as a signalling station to announce the arrival of ships, both friendly and hostile, to the harbour. The earliest record is of a British garrison signalling post in 1704. Signals were sent from blockhouses until 1900, when Cabot Tower took over. Merchant firms had their own house flags to mark property and ships. The approach of commercial shipping became the most important part of the signalling system, with the flags of individual merchants being flown from a mast on Cabot Tower until 1958 to indicate the arrival of one of their ships. Signals gave crews time to get dock facilities ready and call crews to unload the incoming ships.

Cabot Tower, located high upon Signal Hill, was constructed in 1897 to observe the 400th anniversary of the discovery of Newfoundland by John Cabot and also to celebrate the 60th year of the reign of Queen Victoria. A little known fact is that another Cabot Tower was constructed about the same time in Bristol, England. The observation deck on the roof of the Tower is an excellent viewing place and was used to fly the signalling flags to indicate the approach of ships.

Marconi received the first transatlantic wireless signal, the letter "S" in Morse code, from England on December 12, 1901 on the top of Signal Hill in a vacant wing of a military barracks used as a hospital. Until recently the Noon Day gun was fired from Cabot Tower to announce the time at midday.

Quarantine Hospitals were located in converted barracks on Signal Hill and used from 1842 till 1892 when they were destroyed by fire. They then moved to other quarters and were known as the Diphtheria and Fever Hospital and the Signal Hill Hospital until 1920.

Courtesy N. Rusted

Cabot Tower and Quarantine Hospital

Marine Hospital was built in Ross's Valley, the area below Signal Hill in 1892 for smallpox victims and also for cholera. Patients from incoming vessels were to be sent to the hospital from the area near Chain Rock and therefore not have to enter the city. The hospital was established by Judge Prowse and afterwards called **Prowse's Folly** as it was too isolated for many patients to reach. All of the hospitals were eventually destroyed by fire.

Today, the **Signal Hill Interpretation Centre** preserves and interprets the history of military fortifications, signalling stations and medical facilities that served and protected St. John's. Audio visual presentations give the military history of St. John's. Signal Hill was made a National Historic Site on May 22, 1958 because of its early fortifications and Seven Year's War battle site. At this time the road was paved and a renovation program initiated which included the restoration of fortifications on the hill. Signal Hill offers a breathtaking view of the city, harbour, Cape Spear and the Atlantic from its lookout and walkways. A drive up the hill at night to see the city with its twinkling lights is magnificent and a must for any visitor. A hiking trail for the adventurous leads from Cabot Tower down the front of the hill to Ross's Valley and around to the small village of the Battery. It also leads in the opposite direction past Ladies Lookout — the highest point — to Quidi Vidi Battery.

George's Pond, on the higher level of Signal Hill is spring fed and connected to the town's water supply. It was once the town's only water supply.

Gibbet Hill—Gibbeting was a relatively common practice in the 17th, 18th and early 19th centuries. The gibbet was used to display a body, which after execution, was usually dipped in boiling tar, wrapped in chains, and hung until it decomposed and fell apart. The first gibbet in St. John's was near the bottom of Prescott Street and moved in 1759 to Gibbet Hill, a prominent point on Signal Hill. This area was formerly named Crows Nest on old maps of St. John's. The bodies were hung in this prominent place as an example of what could happen to lawbreakers. Folklore has it that the bodies were removed from the gibbets, weighed down and dumped into Deadman's Pond. The gibbet was torn down in 1796 to make way for Wallace's Battery.

THE BATTERY—This fishing village within the city has hardly changed since the early days when it contained fish flakes and sheds used in the fishery, as well as homes of many fishermen. Its name originated from the guns situated there and on other points of the hills overlooking the Narrows, protecting the port of St. John's from attack by pirates and warships. This area has become a popular place to live because of its harbour view and village atmosphere. Its brightly coloured houses have been dubbed "jellybean row" in advertising for the city.

MAGGOTY COVE—The extreme east end of old St. John's, in front of the Standard Manufacturing Company on Water Street, was known as Maggoty Cove. It contained large numbers of fish flakes where fish was made or cured. With an outbreak of poor weather, fish, especially caplin, produced maggots. Those that fell through the boughs or long sticks from the flakes to the path or road below gave the name to this historic part of town. When the flakes were taken down the name of the area was changed to Hoyles Town, after a prominent premier and Chief Justice of the time, Sir Hugh Hoyles.

MONKEY'S PUZZLE—The winding path under the long sticks supporting the fish flakes at Maggoty Cove, which led from the foot of Signal Hill, was called Monkey's Puzzle. Some say that people lived in this area under the flakes.

Unveiling of the War Memorial in St. John's, by Field Marshall Haig, July 1st, 1924

KING'S BEACH—*The War Memorial* is situated adjacent to the site where Sir Humphrey Gilbert landed to claim Newfoundland for England in 1583. The memorial was unveiled by Field Marshall Haig on July 1 1924 on the 8th anniversary of the Battle of the Somme to commemorate the Newfoundlanders who died in the First World War. Engravings were later added to remember those who served and died in World War II. The area of the War Memorial was known as Haymarket, for activities that took place there. Today restaurants and a bar are located nearby in a renovated building named Haymarket Square.

ROTTEN ROW—This site of one of the old fishing rooms was located on northeast Water Street near Springdale Street.

THE REGATTA—The regatta at Quidi Vidi Lake, starting in 1826, is one of the oldest annual sporting events in North America. It is held on the first Wednesday in August, weather permitting. It brings a full day of team races on the "pond" in racing shells, amid much friendly rivalry. The day is a municipal holiday and throngs of people line the lake to view the races and enjoy the festivities.

SOUTHSIDE HILLS—The hills are of a higher elevation than Signal Hill, both protecting the harbour from the fury of the Atlantic Ocean and providing natural fortification against enemy attack.

Fishing rooms, stages, wharves and warehouses were located there until the twentieth century when the south side began to emerge as an industrial area of St. John's with seal and oil factories, docks to load and unload coal, fish and salt. There were almost 1300 residents in 1911, and Imperial Oil and Newfoundland Light and Power moved there. Population continued to rise into the 1940s. The Canadian Army built two barracks during World War II, tanks were built into the hills and houses torn down to improve docking. The population began to decline and when the harbour was reconstructed many houses were torn down between 1959 and 1964 when the hill was dynamited to widen the road and for fill for the reconstruction. Residents still live in the area closest to the Narrows.

During the reconstruction, St. Mary's Church was torn down and a piece of Newfoundland history was lost. Shandithit, the last of the Beothuk Indians, was buried there. Beothuks were the first known inhabitants of Newfoundland. Hunters and fishers, they came to the coast in the spring to catch fish, seals, salmon and gather eggs. They wintered in the interior hunting herds of caribou. The long held theory is that with European settlement, they found it difficult to come to the coastline and became extinct, either starved or suffered from

European diseases.Shandithit was found in 1823, near starving, and brought to St. John's by trappers from the Exploits Bay area. She died six years later.

A monument stands near the site of the old church, on what is believed to be the believed burial site of Shandithit.

The Coast Guard Regional Agency is located on this side of the harbour, a refuelling centre for boats, a Marine Institute training centre and dock, a former fish plant and a power sub station. Oil storage tanks are situated high upon the hill, away from the city. Old metal doors on the base of the hill lead to caves where gunpowder was stored and later liquor aged for the Newfoundland Liquor Corporation.

PROSSER'S ROCK SMALL BOAT BASIN—The federal government moved the small fishing boats from the end of the harbour to their new location n the Narrows at a cost of seven million dollars. The old basin at Riverhead frequently silted up and was becoming crowded with fishermen. The new addition caused much controversy about whether it would affect the environment and natural flushing of the harbour.

CAPE SPEAR—The most easterly point in North America, Cape Spear is but a short distance by car from St. John's, and can be seen from by boat during a tour outside the harbour. The light house at Cape Spear is the oldest existing lighthouse in New-foundland. It was built in 1835 and in service until 1955, manned by the Cantwell family. The lighthouse is now a museum and displays the 19th century dwelling of the lightkeeper and his family. The original light had seven great lenses and reflectors, lit by whale oil lamps. Cape Spear was of strategic importance during World War II with coastal battery fortifications built against the threat of U-boats, to defend the entrance of St. John's harbour. The two large gun emplacements can be still seen there. The panoramic view is magnificent at Cape Spear National Historic Park. One can look out at the endless Atlantic, see Signal Hill and the entrance to St. John's harbour, watch the seabirds, and look for whales and icebergs in season. You are closer, at this point, to Europe than to the centre of Canada.

SPRIGG'S POINT is a black-legged kittiwake bird sanctuary. The looming rocky shoreline is the nesting ground of these small swallow winged seagulls that lay their eggs on narrow ledges and in crevices. A sailboat tour from the St. John's Harbour sails by the spectacular rock formations to observe and listen to these birds in their natural habitat.

THE RAILWAY--St. John's original railway station was on the site of Fort William near the present Hotel Newfoundland. The first rail line ran along what is now Empire Avenue -- the old track. There was also a spur line at Hoyles Town in the east end at the present site of the "Army dock". The 1898 contract with the Reid Newfoundland Company centralized all operations in the west end of St. John's harbour. Railway and machine sheds were moved from Whitbourne to St. John's and a new rail line was built in the west end to replace the old track on Empire Avenue. A new railway station, constructed of granite, was built in 1910 at the west end of Water Street. The area was adjacent to a large pond divided by a bridge and part of St. John's harbour. A large part of the area was later filled in to extend the rail lines and build sheds. The Victorian station is now the home of the CN bus terminal, with the old statue "Woman of Industry" still

Courtesy PANL

An early photograph of the railway station on Water Street West

standing at the front. The Reid Newfoundland Company operated the railway until 1923 when the government took over operation of the rail line and coastal shipping.

The railway was known to locals as the "Newfie Bullet," because of its lack of speed. People were known to get off at the front of the train, pick some berries and get back on again at the caboose at the end! The 537 mile, 1100 kilometre trip across the island from St. John's to Port aux Basques took 27 hours. Completed in 1898, the rail lines were built with light narrow gauge rails, enabling the trains to make tight turns in the steep, rocky areas. These rails did not permit the faster speeds or larger loads of the wider gauge railroads on the mainland. The railway, in accordance with the Terms of Union with Confederation with Canada was to be kept up, but sadly came to an end in July 1969 as it had become uneconomical to operate. The final trip was on September 20, 1988 and work began on dismantling the old narrow gauge rail lines. The rail beds are now mainly used for all-terrain vehicles, snow mobiles and recreational purposes.

BOWRING PARK is located in the west end of the city on Waterford Bridge Road. The land was donated to St. John's by the Bowrings – one of the city's most prominent business families. The park was opened in 1914 to commemorate the centennial of Bowring Brothers Limited. The park contains three interesting bronze statues, two of which are memorials to the World War I dead of the Royal Newfoundland Regiment.

Peter Pan – "In memory of Betty Munn, a dear little girl who loved the park."

The Fighting Newfoundlander is a full life-sized statue of a soldier in full battle kit in the act of throwing a grenade. *The Caribou,* a life sized statue of the emblem of the Regiment, is a replica of a statue at Beaumont Hamel in France. *Peter Pan* was given to the park by Sir Edgar Bowring in memory of his godchild who was drowned at sea. The bronze statue is an exact replica, from the same mould, of the original in Kensington Gardens, London.

RENNIES RIVER HIKING TRAIL—The scenic trail extends from The Freshwater Centre at Pippy Park to Quidi Vidi lake and picturesque Quidi Vidi village. Its pathways and boardwalks follow along the river and offer an enjoyable outing through the centre of the city.

PIPPY PARK, the largest park in the city covering 1343 acres, is located on Mount Scio and Nagles Hill behind the university complex, next to Confederation Building. The park is protected from new construction. It contains a fully serviced campsite and trailer park within the city limits, picnic grounds, hiking trails, the Freshwater Centre, a golf course and the Oxen Pond Botanical Gardens – a 110 acre nature reserve with colourful gardens, trails and native plant collections. In the winter the roads and trails of the campsite are used for cross country skiing and one can skate on Long Pond. St. John's is one of the few cities where this winter activity can be done so close to home!

NEWFOUNDLAND FRESHWATER RESOURCE CENTRE—The centre has a 25 metre fluvarium, a series of underwater viewing windows built into the bed of Nagle's Hill Brook, where one can see a panoramic view of underwater stream life in its natural environment. This lovely octagonal wooden building, the only public fluvarium in North America, is located on the shore of Long Pond in Pippy Park, off Higgin's Line near the Confederation Building. The facility is a project of the Quidi Vidi/Rennies River Development Foundation and is open year round.

CHAPTER FOUR

Surrounded By Water

NEWFOUNDLAND is the tenth largest island in the world, larger than Ireland and slightly smaller than England. Its area is 42,000 square miles, 316 miles in length from north to south, 317 miles from east to west, about one eighth of its area is water. There is approximately 6,000 miles of coastline. Newfoundland is situated in the Gulf of St Lawrence at the "gateway to Canada." It is on the same latitude as Paris, France, but its weather leads one to believe that it is further north.

THE NEWFOUNDLAND CLIMATE

The meeting of two ocean currents determines the island's climate. The Labrador current flowing from the Arctic to Newfoundland via Labrador and the Gulf stream flowing in a northerly direction from the Equator to eastern North America meet off the south coast of Newfoundland. The warm current meeting the cold Arctic current produces a cooling effect and usually fog, the cause of many wrecks and great loss of life in the past. Nowadays radar is essential for ships and fishing boats in this area with some of the worst fogs in the world.

Newfoundland is famous for its unsettled weather. The wind can change at will, and it is said that four seasons could occur in one day. The climate is temperate, cooled in summer and moderated in winter by winds, with rare weather below zero. The annual rainfall in St. John's is about 62 inches. The average yearly temperature recorded is around 40.8 F with a high of 86 F and a low of -10 F. There is snow from January to about April. Spring is almost nonexistent with summer suddenly arriving in May or June. Drift ice occasionally fills St. John's harbour during March, April and May. This has happened twice since 1949 to the point that the harbour was unable to be used for navigation.

NEWFOUNDLAND'S FISHERY

Newfoundland was discovered by Europeans at a time when many countries wanted fish, an important source of protein. The sea at the time was reported to be swarming with so many fish that they could not only be taken in nets, but in baskets let down with a stone. John Cabot, in 1497, said that the cod were so thick that they slowed down the progress of his ship.

From a steel engraving in *The Graphic*, October 17, 1891 – Fishing for cod from a dory.

In those early years, the fishing season and voyage to and from the banks kept early European fishermen away from home for lengthy periods. The two main types of fishery were the *wet* or *green fishery* and the *dry fishery*. The green fishermen salted the caught fish right on board the ships. When they returned home the fish was still in its wet or green condition, then washed, dried and salted. The French, Portuguese and Spanish traditionally used this method. It was not necessary to come ashore as often as the dry fishermen, who had to build stages and flakes on shore to clean and cure the catch.

Stacking fish using a two-man hand barrow .

Fishermen came in sailing ships and caught fish by hand over the side until about the 20th century. Handlining was difficult and labour intensive work. Fishermen often stood in barrels tied to the deck of the ship, for protection and support from the wind and weather. Each fisherman had a pair of handlines about 100 metres long with one or two hooks, and a weight. The entire line had to be hauled up when a fish was hooked. Fifty quintals, or five thousand pounds of fish, was a man's work for the summer.

A more efficient method of fishing was adopted in the 1850s when the fishermen instead went from their ships in small dories and set trawls or longlines with their hundreds of hooks. The crew were able to fish a much larger area. A dory is a flat bottomed boat developed for the inshore fishery. It was ideal for the bank fishery as it could be stacked on the decks of a schooner to save space. It was also very seaworthy and could carry large loads of fish.

Fishing was the main source of income for Newfoundland settlers and the inshore fishing ground became overcrowded. Small schooners brought the colonial fishermen to the offshore banks. The catch could be lightly salted as they were not far from home. On return to port the fish was unloaded from the ship's hold with fish forks, washed to remove dirt and excess salt, then piled to press out excess moisture. It was then spread on large flakes to dry in the sun. When the fish was partially dry it was piled again to press out more moisture. This was repeated until the fish was properly preserved. The fish was sorted by size and quality and packed in barrels or stored in bulk. Bulk fish were dried again in the sun before being exported.

CODFISH

Cod was an important food staple in the days before refrigeration. The flesh could be preserved either by drying or by salting. Dried cod kept well and was less expensive than meat. Consequently it gained a wide market in hot countries, especially amongst the poor.

Atlantic cod has been one of the major fish resources of Canada, and "fish" in Newfoundland always means codfish. The species of northern cod has supplied about three quarters of all the fish landed in Newfoundland and Labrador. Today, even with the stock in serious trouble and fishermen looking to other species, the northern cod remains the most important stock in our waters.

Fisheries managers study the habits and features of different stocks – their migration, spawning, growth patterns and life span. Tagging is one method of studying fish movement. Scientists then rely on fishermen to return any tags found on fish caught. Each tag supplies information on where and when the fish was tagged and where and when it was caught, helping to build up a picture of the movement of different fish stocks. Cod in southerly waters grow faster than the same fish living in colder waters farther north. A few fish stray far from their home waters. A cod tagged off northern Europe in 1957 was caught off Newfoundland , more than 2000 miles away, in 1961.

Cod spawn offshore in winter and spring, normally in deep water, and spawning information is known only from behaviour studied in tanks. Northerly cod tend to spawn earlier than those further south, perhaps due to slower development in colder waters. After spawning, the eggs gradually rise to the surface and drift with the current. How many survive at this stage depends largely on where the current takes them. Cod lay millions of eggs, but only a few from each pair survive. Each cod that reaches maturity escaping all the dangers in its existence is truly one in a million.

The codfish lays a million eggs,
The homely hen lays one,
But the codfish never cackles
To tell you when she's done.
And so we scorn the codfish
While the humble hen we prize,
Which only goes to show that
It pays to advertise.   *Anon.*

CAPLIN

Caplin, similar to sardine, are most abundant in Canada in areas around Newfoundland and Labrador. Most live on banks offshore and spawn on beaches or gravel shoals near the shore. Spawning takes place in early June and July when mature caplin move towards the beaches. Females usually release all of their eggs at one time, on an average of 4600. Males may mate more than once but most caplin die after spawning. The eggs stick to sand or gravel and hatch in 15 to 20 days. The larvae stay

Loading caplin into a box cart.

Courtesy PANL

in the gravel until washed out by the waves, return to offshore banks to feed on plankton and take 3 or 4 years to mature.

Newfoundland's commercial caplin fishery supplies roe-bearing female fish to Japan. The catch is valuable and therefore an important commercial species. Caplin are also an important forage fish in the North West Atlantic, fed upon by seabirds, seals, whales, haddock, flounder, salmon, herring and most of all by cod.

The "Caplin scull" usually takes place in late June or early July. Schools of spawning caplin are driven into shallow water by codfish and ashore by the tides. It is said locally that the caplin are rolling ashore. Each year Newfoundlanders look forward to the caplin run and go to the beaches to watch the activity, catch caplin to eat or for fertilizer in their gardens. The caplin are hand picked from the beach, or caught in cast nets.

Unfortunately in recent years the caplin scull is not as plentiful as it used to be.

TRADITIONAL FISHING GEAR IN NEWFOUNDLAND

JIGGER—The traditional jigger is lead and the Norwegian jigger made of stainless steel. No bait is needed; the jigger is lowered almost to the bottom and then drawn up and down. Cod are lured and may be caught by the head, body or tail.

HANDLINE—The hook is usually baited with squid. A series of hooks with artificial bait are sometimes also attached to the line. A heavy lead weight is used to keep the bait near the bottom. Fishermen frequently had a line on each side of the boat.

TRAWLS OR LONG LINES—Trawls have many short lines attached at regular intervals. Each short line has a hook which is usually baited with squid. Trawls are placed on the bottom with a small anchor at each end and marked by buoys. They are hauled to the boat to remove the fish and usually coiled in tubs to be rebaited ashore. Each line is 50 fathoms long and 20 to 30 lines are often set together.

DEEP-SEA TRAWLS—Introduced in the 1930s, deep-sea trawls are very large net bags lowered in to the water from the back of stern trawlers and the sides of side trawlers. The ships are connected to the nets by two cables – one from each side of the opening of the bag which is hauled along behind the trawler gathering everything in its path. The trawl is hauled on board, emptied of its catch and returned to the water.

SALMON NETS are made of nylon with many small floats along the top and with a lead foot rope. It is kept on the surface with large buoys and held in place by heavy anchors. Salmon are caught by their gills and removed without taking the net from the water. Nets are usually 50 fathoms long.

GILL NETS are similar in construction to salmon nets. They are made of monofilament and sunk to the bottom by small weights. The ends are marked by buoys. The nets are hauled into the boats to remove the fish and then reset in the water. Three or four nets are often set together. Nets are 50 fathoms long and 1 fathom deep.

COD TRAPS—A cod trap is like a mesh box with a floor resting on the bottom. The top is held up by many small floats and large buoys from the corners, sides and back. Each of these is secured by a heavy anchor. The codfish are diverted into the door of the trap, as they follow caplin, by the leader which projects from the door towards the shore. The size and shape of traps vary, the average being 60 fathoms around and with a 50 fathom leader.

They are usually hauled twice a day by a crew working from a trap boat aided by a dory. First the door is closed by hauling up a rope attached to the bottom front. Then the front corners are hauled up and the fish are gradually collected along one side or the back by hauling in the mesh bottom. The catch is taken into the boat by a dipnet.

THE SCHOONER—A sailing vessel is referred to by her rigging, which defines an arrangement of masts, spars, yards and sails. A schooner is described as a ship having two gaff sails, the fore being larger than the after sail, and a head sail. The two masted schooner was developed in New England around 1700. The fore and aft sails could be manipulated from the deck making schooners more manageable than square rigged vessels. The early schooners were only about 60 feet long and had a crew of 10 or 12. The original vessels on the American coast were called catches and shallops. The name schooner appeared early in the 18th century, coming about by the peculiar skipping motion, or "scooning," made by the smaller sailing vessels.

The influence of schooners developed in the American colonies during this period spread northwards into Nova Scotia, New Brunswick, Prince Edward Island, Newfoundland and Labrador. The schooner needed only a small crew in proportion to its size, and was ideal for the westerly prevailing winds along the east coast of North America. It was also made popular by its ability at sea during the winter. Frost and ice made navigation difficult and the crew was able to do all their work on deck in the freezing weather, instead of aloft as was necessary on the larger ships.

The "Fisherman" schooner, introduced in 1900 by Mr. B.B. Crowninshield, a Boston yacht designer, had short, straight keels, raking stern posts, long overhanging counters and a cut away forefoot. These changes formed a break at the forward end of the keel and a curved sweep to the stem head. The fisherman profile included a full two masted schooner rig with a bowsprit, similar to that of the famous *Bluenose*, and was widely used in Newfoundland.

Sailing schooner

LIFE IN A FISHING SCHOONER

The fishing season opened in March and continued until October. Most vessels made about two or three trips to the banks during that period. Each trip was about three weeks but could be as long as eight weeks if the fishing was poor. The schooner had a small forward cabin, where most of the men slept, cooked and ate. The captain and a few of the men lived in an aft cabin. The two fish holds took up most of the space on the boat. The provisions were kept in the bilges below the galley to keep cool.

Long hours of hard work were part of life at sea, work starting before daylight and continuing until late at night. There was a cycle of baiting, fishing, bringing the fish on board and

Steel engraving of work below decks in a banking schooner – from *The Graphic*, October 17, 1891.

cleaning and storing it in the hold. Men were often lost in the fog in their dories; sometimes they were recovered but often were not. It was said that two standard traditions for most fishermen were that it was unlucky to work on Sunday and useless for a fisherman to learn to swim as he would not be able to survive far from land in the cold Atlantic waters. Another saying was that a man who would go to sea for a living would go to hell for a pastime. Many suffered badly from the elements but knew no other way of life. The Grand Bank fishery was one of great hazards, long distances and lengths of time away from home. Tragedy often struck with fog or storms separating dories and men from their ships.

There was an ongoing tradition of boat building in Newfoundland, with its roots in its British ancestry, which in many areas developed into an industry. The tradition was passed from father to son in an informal manner. New designs such as the Western or Jack Schooner, Bully Boat, Fisherman and Banking Schooner gradually became adapted to suit Newfoundland conditions.

Most transportation and travel in Newfoundland was by schooner between the far flung coastal communities. The sea was the principal highway for most Newfoundland outports. Coastal boats and schooners moved passengers and freight in the only possible way among the scattered coves and villages along the vast coastline. Most people lived close to the sea, depended on the sea for a livelihood and relied on boats as their only link to the outside world. Boats were indispensable elements of fishing, transportation, communication and commerce.

THE COLLAPSE OF THE RESOURCE BASE

The Harris report — Recommendations of the Independent Review Panel on Northern Cod, released in 1990 — stated that "Northern cod stocks have been exploited by fishermen since c.1481. Although these patterns have varied, these stocks were, for at least four hundred years, the economic foundation for growth of a settled community along the east and northeast coasts of Newfoundland and the coast of Labrador. Though supplemented by comparatively modest contributions from other marine species such as salmon, herring, seals and whales, the cod stocks were the raison d'etre for the existence of Newfoundland as a colony."

The fishery has been the basis of Newfoundland's economy for centuries, and now the resource base of the fishery — the cod stocks on the Grand Banks — has essentially collapsed. The outlook is grim for the Atlantic fishery. A moratorium or closure of commercial fishing was established on 2 July 1992 by the Government of Canada, and may have to be in effect for years to come. This has had consequences of a social, political and economic nature. It had a drastic affect on the economy, causing great uncertainty about the future and affecting the lives of thousands of people. Many have had their only means of livelihood taken away from them. It has meant a loss of employment and income for 12,000 fishermen and 15,000 plant workers, as well as 1200 others affected by the impact upon Fishery Products International and other large operations. In reality one half of these may never work in the fishery again.

NCARP – the Northern Cod Adjustment and Recovery Program, and AGAP – the Atlantic Groundfish Adjustment Program, were implemented as income assistance to aid fishermen and plant workers until May 14, 1994, until decisions were made. TAGS — The Atlantic Groundfish Strategy — replaced NCARP and AGAP on 16 May 1994. This was designed to decrease dependence on the fishery but it is not the solution to the problem.

ALTERNATIVE FISHERIES

THE SCALLOP FISHERY—With the downturn in groundfish stocks interest has turned to other species such as crab and scallops. Interest in the scallop fishery has grown and will grow as long as the price is high. It has been a Godsend for some fishermen. The invertebrate catch value has been over 50% of the total catch value landed in the last few years. If the catch by other countries is included this figure rises to 60%. The cuts in the TAC — Total Allowable Catch — for traditional species,

The Scallop Fishery

along with the cod Moratorium have created a need for the development of a new species. Pound for pound the scallop is the most lucrative fish on the Grand Banks.

The *Icelandic scallop* is considered a sedentary species as it is attached to the bottom by filaments. It is smaller than the *Sea scallop* and is more labour intensive to shuck or shell. The Icelandic scallop was once considered a nuisance species, but now with high prices and the quality product on the Grand Banks the demand is high.

The Grand Banks, on the continental shelf off Newfoundland, consist of an area about three times as large as Newfoundland and Labrador, approximately 60,000 square miles, with less than 100 fathoms of depth in the water. Due to the meeting of the Labrador current and the Gulf stream the area is rich in plankton – a rich food for fish. The area around

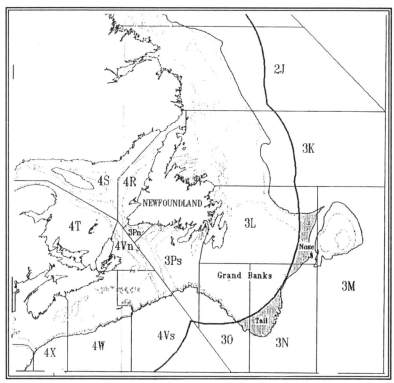

200 Mile Fishing Zone and NAFO Fishing Boundaries.

Lily and Carson Canyons on the fringe of the Banks is one of the most lucrative fishing areas. The canyons were the site of much of the filming of Tom Clancy"s "Hunt for Red October" starring Sean Connery.

The decline of stocks in the traditional scallop fishing grounds caused Nova Scotia fishermen to come east in the 1950s looking for sea scallops. They found Icelandic scallops but these took more effort to shuck so they confined their interest to the Saint Pierre Banks. The Canadian fleet was effectively banned from the St. Pierre Bank with the introduction of a new twenty-four mile limit in the French zone. In the late 1980s the Icelandic scallop began to be fished. The Straits of Belle Isle had only sea scallops; the St. Pierre Bank fishery begun in 1989-90 had a mixture of sea and Icelandic, and the Grand Banks started in 1992 had only Icelandic. Fishermen and researchers are still trying to define species aggregations in certain areas. (Icelandic scallops were fished minimally on the Grand Banks 50 years ago.)

This new fishery has caused a return to the old small wooden boats and hazard to fishermen 200 miles from shore on the Grand Banks. Not all boats with scallop licences have the capability to fish offshore so only a small number can take advantage of the opportunity. Boats are being refitted for this new venture. The harbour in St. John's has become a centre of activity when the boats return after their 1-2 weeks at sea for repairs and supplies. The small 30-60 metre long vessels are normally equipped with stabilizers on each side that are lowered while at sea to increase stability. The vessels are equipped with hoists and drags. The drags, used to rake the bottom for scallops, are hoisted and the shellfish unloaded onto shucking tables located on the back side sections of the boat. The scallops are shucked as soon as they are caught, the meat removed and iced to preserve it as trips can last up to 14 days at sea. The shells are disposed of over the side of the boat by lifting up the hinged tables. The fishery is labour intensive with very long hours worked while at sea.

THE CRAB FISHERY—Crab contributes about 200 million to Newfoundland's once cod dependent economy. Queen crab or "snow crab" was once considered to be a nuisance species by Newfoundland fishermen. They began to be fished commercially in 1969 with dramatic increases in landings since then.

Crab boats range from around 50 feet to a maximum of 65 feet and carry a five or six man crew. Crab are caught in baited conical crab pots, 48" in diameter at the bottom, 28" at the top and 24" high. The pot is emptied into the boat hold and sorted for size into boxes. The pots are rebaited and set again in "fleets" in the water. The undersized crab are returned to the ocean. At the end of a two or three day trip the chilled boxed crab are taken to a plant for processing.

WHO'S WHO IN NEWFOUNDLAND WATERS

The Hooded, Ringed, Harp, Gray, Bearded and Harbour **seals** live in Newfoundland and Labrador. Harp seals spend the summer in the Arctic and migrate to Newfoundland waters in late fall, giving birth to their pups on the pack ice in the early spring. They gather in large concentrations to shed their fur east of Belle Isle, then move back north.

The Seal Fishery--Sealing was a traditional part of Newfoundland's economy, at first for the seal oil, then for pelts for leather and fur, and the meat. Sealing helped diversify the economy and encourage permanent settlement. Much of northern Newfoundland was populated in areas such as Fogo, Greenspond and Bonavista because of sealing in the spring, trapping fur, fishing salmon in the early summer and the summer fishery.

Sealing was part of the scene in St. John's in the 19th and early 20th centuries. The first ships sailed to the ice from St. John's in 1795. The hunt expanded rapidly and after 1800 over 100 of the small vessels carried between 3500 and 4000 to the ice each spring. Many spin off industries developed from the hunt. Seal oil factories were located on the Southside of St. John's harbour. The northern seal hunt took place annually in March and April when hundreds of men flocked to St. John's to get a "berth" on one of the sealing ships to the "front" – the breeding ground of the harp and hood seals located on the pack ice off northern Newfoundland and southeastern Labrador. The harbour in St. John's would be crowded with people watching the blessing of the fleet, and its departure from the harbour with great fanfare and sirens blowing.

The seal hunt was a dangerous occupation and many men and vessels were lost at sea or on the ice. There is no longer a commercial offshore hunt. Newfoundland lost its sealing tradition and hunt in 1970 when international animal welfare groups won their protest against the hunt. Today, with a mall quota, the hunt is carried out in small boats near the shore. The impact of seals on the cod stocks has caused worry, especially since the end of the commercial hunt. Scientists are studying this difficult question, but, it is not easy to estimate the effects on the fishery. **Basking sharks** are quite common in Newfoundland. They are the second largest fish in the world, not dangerous but sometimes harmful to inshore fishermen when they collide with nets. Much of the damage to inshore fishing gear by basking sharks is blamed on whales. The sharks' dorsal and tail fins are brownish coloured and can be seen where the basking sharks "bask" on the surface of the water on calm days. Adults range from 20-30 feet and have very rough skin, baleen which strain plankton and food from the water, and tiny teeth. Basking sharks are distinguished from other common sharks in Newfoundland waters by their large size, baleen, and huge gill arches. They look a little like whales on the surface, but whales move more quickly than basking sharks, breathe on the surface and are warm blooded. Basking sharks' brains are the size of golf balls, while that of the whale is larger than man's. The basking shark swims along with its mouth open to feed, straining plankton from the water with its baleen. It doesn't catch caplin or other fish as it swims too slowly. It hibernates on the bottom in winter due to the low plankton abundance at this time. The adult basking shark averages 24 feet in length and the juvenile 13 feet.

Whales—There about twenty different species of whales in Newfoundland. Whales are mammals, breathe air, produce their young alive, nurse them on milk, and have developed to survive entirely in water. Whale watching is an exciting experience and is possible in the St. John's area during the months of June to August from Signal Hill, Cape Spear and on some of the boat tours departing from St. John's Harbour. Whales can be identified by their size, dorsal fins, the shape of their blow when they come up for air, or as in the case of the humpback whale, its flukes when it dives.

Most **humpback whales** are seen from May – September, but most commonly in the summer months when food is more plentiful. They range in length from 35 – 40 feet long, the young from 25 feet and the female 3 – 4 feet longer than the male. Humpbacks are noted for their long white flippers, which are about one third of their body length, and wart-like knobs on their heads. Their blow is a bushy balloon shape; the back is usually then seen. After about 5-10 blows a final dive is often seen, with tail flukes seen clearly above the water. Fluke patterns on the tail are used to identify individual animals, like fingerprints in humans.

Spectacular acrobatics are associated with the humpback.

They can leap into the air, lie on their sides and roll, waving and slapping their flippers into the air and water, they also can raise their tails into the air and repeatedly slap the water. These behaviours make the humpback a thrilling animal to watch.

Fin whales are commonly seen from early spring until late fall, and travel in groups of 2-8. The blow is long and column shaped and there may be 5-8 blows before the whale dives again. Unlike the humpback, the fin whale does not show its flukes when beginning a dive.

The **minke** is a common whale in Newfoundland and Labrador during the summer and fall. It is seen mostly on its own and usually close to shore, but may be found further out and in small groups. The whales are black on top with white bellies. Their blows are close to the surface and difficult to see.

Seabirds—The Newfoundland coastline is home to many species of seabirds — puffins, gannets, black-legged kittiwakes, Atlantic turres, storm petrels, northern razorbills, cormorants, southern black guillemots and herring gulls. Several of the more than 400 puffin colonies in Newfoundland are the largest on the continent of North America and the three gannet colonies amongst the second largest. Boat tours out of St. John's and Bay Bulls on the Southern Shore view many of these birds in their natural environment. Thousands can be seen soaring in the air or perched on the rugged cliffs. You will be amazed by the sight and sounds. A day trip to Cape St. Mary's bird sanctuary is a splendid outing to see puffins. Bird Rock is the second largest nesting place for gannets in North America. The sanctuaries provide great opportunities to photograph these seabirds.

LOOKING TO THE FUTURE: HIBERNIA DEVELOPMENT

Oil and gas were discovered on the Grand Banks in 1979 and the Binding Agreement was signed September 14, 1990. The Hibernia oilfield, named for a ship called the S.S. Hibernia which helped lay communications cable between Heart's Content Newfoundland and Ireland in the 1800s, is located 315 km. off the coast of Newfoundland on the eastern edge of the Grand

Building on a Solid Base

• Total height of platform: 218 m • Total weight of platform: 1,270,000 t • Topsides Dimensions: 154 m long x 84 m wide x 114 m high • Topsides weight: 58,000 t • Concrete Gravity Base Structure height: 111 m • GBS diameter: 106 m • GBS total weight: 1,220,000 t

Banks in 80 metres of water. The Hibernia Management and Development Company Ltd. is an operating company to oversee the construction and production phases of the Hibernia project formed by the owner companies: Mobil Oil Canada Properties (33.125%); Chevron Canada Resources (26.875%); Petro-Canada Hibernia Partnership (25%); Murphy Atlantic Offshore Oil Company (6.5%); and Canada Hibernia Holding Corporation (8.5%).

The Hibernia oil production facility will include a concrete pedestal or Gravity Base Structure (GBS), the Topsides oil production facilities, a crude oil loading system, and two purpose built shuttle tankers. Two production reservoirs are located in the Hibernia oil field: the Hibernia sandstones and the Avalon sandstones. More than 600 million barrels of oil are expected to be recovered. Production drilling, scheduled for 1997, with a total of 83 development wells, should average 125,000 barrels a day over the life of the project and will represent 12% of Canada's total oil production.. Pre-production cost of the project is to be approximately $5.8 billion Canadian.

The Gravity Base system has been used in the North Sea, an environment similar to Newfoundland. Construction of the GBS, assembly of completed topsides, and the mating of the GBS with the topsides will take place at Mosquito Cove in Bull Arm, Trinity Bay on the northeast coast of Newfoundland, 130 km. northwest of St. John's. Construction began at Bull Arm in October 1990. The 4,000 acre construction site is a small fully serviced town for more than 3,400 people and at the end of construction will be turned over to the Newfoundland Government for one dollar. The 120,000 tonne GBS was towed on November 14 1994 from the dry dock area to the deep water construction site where the second phase of construction is taking place. The components of the production system will be assembled by July 1996 and the platform will be towed to the oilfield. Development drilling and production are scheduled to begin in 1997.

NEWFOUNDLAND AND THE SEA

Whether through offshore oil exploration, a non-traditional species fishery, or a revival of the traditional cod fishery, the sea which surrounds Newfoundland will always be an integral part of the province's economy. The sea is at the very essence of the life of the province. This is vividly expressed in L.E.F. English's *Historic Newfoundland* with a quote by Lt. Col. William Wood, a prominent Canadian author and historian:

> Newfoundland is an island of the sea if ever there was one. Nowhere else does the sea enter so intimately into the life of a people – calling, always calling them – loudly along a thousand miles of surf washed coastline, echoing up a hundred resounding fiords that search out the very heart of the land, whispering through a thousand little tickles, – but calling, always calling its sons away to the fishing grounds and sometimes to the very seafaring ends of the earth.

CHAPTER FIVE

NEWFOUNDLAND TRIVIA

Many famous people have visited St. John's. **Captain Cook,** the Pacific explorer, mapped much of Newfoundland's coastline during the years 1763-67. **Captain Bligh** of the *Bounty* visited the Harbour. **Marconi** sent his first wireless message across the Atlantic in 1901 from Signal Hill, using kites to keep his antennas aloft in the high winds. **Alcock and Brown** left St. John's from Lester's Field on Blackmarsh Road on June 14, 1919, and flew the first successful transatlantic flight to Clifden,

Courtesy PANL — A-50

Alcock and Brown's Vickers-Vimi leaving St. John's on June 14, 1919.

County Galway, Ireland. The flight in the Vikers-Vimy took sixteen hours and twelve minutes! **Lindberg** flew through the Narrows on his solo flight to Paris in 1927. More recently, prominent people served with the US forces at Fort Pepperrell – **John Williams** scored his first movie in St. John's, a tourist promotion for the Newfoundland government, actor/comedian **Bill Cosby** served at Argentia and **The Four Aces**, a popular singing group in the 1950s, began their career in Newfoundland.

One of the most important inventions of World War I, **the gas mask,** was invented in Newfoundland in 1915 by Cluny MacPherson, a medical doctor.

The **first Smallpox vaccination** in North America was performed by Dr. John Clinch in Trinity in 1798. He was a friend and colleague of Dr. Edward Jenner – who discovered the smallpox vaccine in England.

Newfoundland can still be considered a "nursery for seamen" as thirty percent of the Canadian Navy are Newfoundlanders.

At the outbreak of World War Two in 1939, eighty German nationals were taken as prisoners of war from ships at Botwood, and placed in an internment camp constructed at Pleasantville in St. John's. They were transferred to Western Canada in 1941.

A battery operated automatic German weather station was placed in a remote area of Labrador on October 23, 1943. It was not found until recently. The U-boats log reported that it only transmitted data for two weeks!

Newfoundland was the British Empire's first colony and the tenth province of Canada.

Labrador became part of Newfoundland in 1763 after the Seven Years War.

BELIEVE IT OR NOT
(from the Fisheries and Oceans Fisherman's Calendar)

Newfoundland's biggest cod: George Earle, Carbonear, caught a 150 lb. cod by jigger off Spare Harbour, Labrador, in 1949.

Deepest Dive: a forty-seven-foot sperm whale got its jaw caught in a submarine cable that was 620 fathoms deep.

Largest fish caught in Newfoundland: a basking shark caught in Old Perlican. It was thirty-five feet long.

Biggest whale: a ninety-five-foot blue whale weighing over 150 tons.

Oldest Trap Skiff still in use: Eric Strickland of Lamaline uses one built in 1929.

Biggest Pet: Some fishermen on the southern shore feed minke whales.

Worst fogs in the World: on the Grand Banks.

Biggest Tow: C-Core towed icebergs in experiments to test offshore oil platform safety.

Long Fish Life: Cod can live twenty-five to fifty years.

Biggest Reptile: The leatherback turtle can weigh up to 1,500 lbs.

Exceptional Fertility: Female cod can shed between three and nine million eggs at a time, depending upon their size.

Worst Infant Mortality: From all a cod's eggs, only a few survive to adulthood.

Largest "Catch and Release" Program in the World: the Whale Entrapment Assistance Program in Newfoundland and Labrador. In 1991 a total of over five million pounds of humpback whales were released from fishing gear.

❦   ❦   ❦

Unusual Diet: In 1871, a fisherman in St. John's was dressing—the term for cleaning—a large codfish and noticed that the fish had a full stomach which contained shells, fish bones, crab parts and a gold wedding ring with the initials of its owner and a date inside the band. The owner had been a passenger aboard the steamship "Anglo Saxon" which was lost off Chance Cove ... ten years before.

Crime and Punishment: The hanging of the first woman in North America is said to have occurred in St. John's in the 1700s. She and her husband murdered the local magistrate. She was hung and buried on the site of the Royal Trust Building on Water Street and Prescott Street.

A **Barking Kettle** was the name given to a large iron pot in which a mixture of spruce bark and water was boiled. Nets and sails were then immersed in the pot to get a protective coating for longer use in the elements.

A **Killick** is the term used for an anchor made of wood and weighted down with stones. A master seaman in the navy was referred to as a killick – perhaps due to his rank insignia of an anchor. To "dowse the killick" was the term used when throwing the anchor overboard.

A **Quintal** is a measure of fresh, dried or cured fish. It was traditionally measured "by eye," technically a hundredweight, but considered to be 112 pounds to account for inexact calculation, differences in size and spoilage.

Outports are what the villages or small communities outside St. John's and the larger centres are called.

Screeching-in Ceremony: First time visitors to Newfoundland may find themselves participating in an unforgettable ceremony known as a "screech-in" where they sample Newfoundland rum known as **Screech** amid much merriment.

Local Food: Local dishes include Lobster in season, cod tongues, fish and brewis, seal meat, caplin, Jigg's dinner – salt beef and cabbage. Dessert lovers will find Newfoundland's berries to be delicious and distinctive. Partridgeberries, bakeapples and blueberries are the most popular fruit.

Newman's Port: The wine was traditionally shipped from Portugal and aged in cellars built in 1847 on the corner of Springdale and Water Streets. The wine vaults were purchased by the government and declared a provincial historic site in 1986. Newman's Port is now matured in the Kenmount Road plant of the Newfoundland Liquor Corporation and distributed around the world.

Newfoundland Dog: This large distinctive breed is thought to have evolved from dogs brought by Basques fishermen in the 1500s as ship's dogs, crossed with other dogs brought by the British. The Newfoundland is a strong working dog with a predominantly black, double coat of fur, webbed feet, a gentle good companion known for bravery and saving many from drowning. It was also used for carrying mail and first placed on a postage stamp in 1887. The pure-breed Newfoundland dog was saved from extinction by a local breeder, the Hon. Harold MacPherson, at about the beginning of the century when he established Westerland Kennels in St. John's.

The Pitcher Plant (Sarracenis Purpurea): The pitcher plant was declared the provincial flower of Newfoundland in 1954. The unusual plant found mainly in bogs and marshes has a large, single wine-red flower with a red and gold centre and pitcher shaped leaves attached around the bottom of the stem. The hollow leaves fill with water and the insectivorous plant feeds from insects that become trapped inside. Queen Victoria chose the pitcher plant to be engraved on the new Newfoundland penny in the late 1800s.

Newfoundland Flag: For many years Newfoundland used England's flag, the Union Jack, as its symbol, but a provincial flag that was distinctively our own was wanted in the 1970s. Premier Brian Peckford formed a committee in 1979, headed by Artist Christopher Pratt to select a design. The flag was officially described in 1980 by the selection committee as follows:

> In this flag the primary colours of Red, Gold and Blue are placed against a background of white to allow the design to stand out clearly. White is representative of now and ice; blue represents the sea; red represents human effort and gold our confidence in ourselves. The blue section, most reminiscent of the Union Jack represents our commonwealth heritage which has so decisively shaped our present. The red and gold section, larger than the other, represents our future. The two triangles outlined in red portray the mainland and island portions of our province reaching the way to what we believe

will be a bright future. ...the whole flag represents our past, present and future.

The entire flag is one of symbolism – a Christian cross, Beothuk and Naskapi ornamentation, outline of the maple leaf in the centre, image of a trident to emphasize our continued dependence on the fishery and ocean resources. When hung as a banner the arrow takes on the appearance of a sword to remind us of the sacrifice of our war veterans. The design of the flag takes us from our earliest Beothuk beginnings and points forward representing our past, present and future.

Pronunciation of Newfoundland: Rhymes with understand, otherwise you will be marked as an "outsider" or " CFA – come from away"!

Newfoundland Standard Time: Newfoundland time is 3½ hours behind Greenwich Mean Time. It is the only place in North America to have a half hour time zone, one half hour later than Atlantic Time, dating from when it was part of the British Empire. An old joke says that "The world will end at midnight ... 12:30 in Newfoundland!"

Historic Role in Communication & Travel: Newfoundland is closer to Europe than any other North American city, and closer to England than it is to Alberta – half way across Canada. Thus Newfoundland has played a historic role in transatlantic communication and travel. Marconi received the first transatlantic wireless message and St. John's was the departure point for Alcock and Brown who won the prize of $50,000 offered by an English newspaper for the first flight across the Atlantic. Heart's Content was the site of the first successful transatlantic cable landed in 1866 by the ship *Great Eastern*. A major cable relay station was located in Heart's Content for over 100 years and brought many trained and educated people to the island.

Newfoundland Stamps: Newfoundland released about 300 different designs of postage stamps between 1857 and 1949 when replaced by Canadian stamps. Today Newfoundland stamps and covers are collectors items and much sought over at auctions worldwide. They are considered rarities and catalogue prices for many are valued in the tens of thousands of dollars. The stamps are known for their attractive designs and have made many aware of our history and way of life.

Our Culture: Newfoundland has a rich culture of its own. Its songs, recitations and oral history are varied and plentiful. The unusual place names of our communities and natural landmarks are reminders of our forefathers' experiences, roots, imagination and sense of humour. The place names reflect the background of the French, Spanish, Portuguese, Basques and English. These unique and unusual names on our map provide a fascinating study of their origins. We, the people are proud of this heritage and our traditional culture.

Bibliography

Atlantic Provinces in Confederation, The, Forbes, E.R., D.A. Muise, eds. Chap. 10 – "Newfoundland Confronts Canada, 1867 – 1949." Pp 349-381. Dr. James Hillier. University of Toronto Press, 1993.

Briffett, Frances *The Story of Newfoundland and Labrador* Toronto: J.M. Dent and Sons (Canada) Limited, 1954.

Baker, Melvin, *The Government of St. John's, Newfoundland, 1800-1921.* Dept. of History, Faculty of Graduate Studies, The University of Western Ontario, London, Ontario, September 1980.

Bulletin of Canadian Studies, Winter 1983/4, Vol. VII, No. 2 – "The Newfoundland Seal Fishery, An Historical Introduction." Pp 49-67. Dr. James Hillier.

Cell, Gillian T. *English Enterprise in Newfoundland 1577 - 1660.* Toronto: University of Toronto Press, 1969.

Chadwick, St. John. *Newfoundland - Island into Province.* Cambridge: University Press, 1967.

Charting a New Course Towards the Fishery of the Future Report of the Task Force on Incomes and Adjustment in the Atlantic Fishery November 1993, Ottawa, Fisheries and Oceans Communications Directorate, 1993.

Colonial Office Original Correspondence. Board of Trade Newfoundland. *Colonial Office Series 194.* London: Public Record Office.

Davies, Glanville J. *England and Newfoundland: Policy and Trade 1660 - 1783.* Doctorate of Philosophy. Faculty of Arts. Dept of History. University of Southhampton, 1980.

Dept. of Public Works of Canada. *Harbour Survey - St. John's, Newfoundland.* Parts I & II. Fenco. 1957.

Encyclopaedia of Newfoundland and Labrador, Vol. 1, 1981; Vol. 2, 1984; 1st Editions, St. John's: Newfoundland Book Publishers (1967) Limited, Vol. 3, 1991; Vol.4, 1993; Vol. 5, 1994; 1st Editions, St. John's: Harry Cuff Publications Limited.

English, L.E.F., *Historic Newfoundland,* Newfoundland Dept. of Tourism, 1974.

Fisheries and Oceans Canada *Fisheries Calendar 1994.*

Graham, Gerald S. *Fisheries and Seapower.* Canadian Historical Association Annual Report. Ottawa: Canadian Historical Association, 1941.

Greene, John P. *Trial and Triumph: The History of Newfoundland and Labrador*, Toronto: Doubleday Canada Limited, 1982.

Hibernia Management and Development Company Ltd. *Building On A Solid Base*, January, 1995.

Handcock, W. Gordon. *So Long as There Comes Noe Women. Origins of English Settlement in Newfoundland*. History Series 6. St. John's: Breakwater Books, 1989.

MacKay, R.A. *Newfoundland - Economic, Diplomatic and Strategic Studies*. Toronto: Oxford University Press, 1946.

Matthews, Keith. *Lectures on the History of Newfoundland - 1500- 1830*. St. John's: Breakwater Books, 1988.

McLintock, A.H. *The Establishment of Constitutional Government in Newfoundland 1783-1832*. Longmans Green, 1941.

Moakler, L. D. *Ye Olde St. John's: Its Wells, Its Brooks, Its Unfamiliar Names*, Pamphlet.

Newfoundland Royal Commission 1933 Report London: His Majesty's Stationary Office, 1933.

Penney, Gerald Associates Limited South Castle *Deliniation Project -1993* Report of Excavations at Anchor Point. January 1995.

Prowse, D.W. *History of Newfoundland from English, Colonial and Foreign Records*. London: MacMillan and Co, 1985.

Pullen, Rear-Admiral H.F. *Atlantic Schooners* Brunswick Press, 1967.

Rowe, C. Francis, *In Fields Afar - A Review of the Establishment of the Anglican Parish of St. John's and its Cathedral*, St. John's: Seawise Enterprises, 1989.

Rowe, Frederick W. *A History of Newfoundland and Labrador*. Toronto: McGraw-Hill Ryerson Limited, 1980.

Ryan, Shannon. *An Abstract of the CO194 Statistics*. Newfoundland Census Returns.

St. John's: A National Harbours Board Project. K.E. Smith. Filmstrip. MUN Clearinghouse 1977. Historical Information, description of modern day use of St. John's Harbour.

St. John's: A Harbour Reborn. Motion Picture, Ottawa. Crawley Films Ltd. Development and reconstruction of St. John's Harbour.

Whiteley, William. *James Cook in Newfoundland 1762-1767*. Newfoundland Historical Society. Pamphlet Number 3. 1975.

Young, Ewart. Ed. *This is Newfoundland*. Toronto: The Ryerson Press, 1949.